MAKING *Artisan* CHEESE

QUARRY

50 FINE CHEESES THAT YOU CAN MAKE
IN YOUR OWN KITCHEN

BEVERLY MASSACHUSETTS

QUARRY BOOKS

TIM SMITH

First published in the United States of America by
Quayside Publishing Group
100 Cummings Center
Suite 406-L
Beverly, Massachusetts 01915-6101
Telephone: (978) 282-9590
Fax: (978) 283-2742
www.quarrybooks.com

Library of Congress Cataloging-in-Publication Data
Smith, Tim.
    Making artisan cheese : fifty fine cheeses that you can make in your own
kitchen / Tim Smith.
       p.   cm.
    Includes index.
    ISBN 1-59253-197-0 (pbk.)
    1. Cheese. 2. Cheese—Varieties. 3. Cookery (Cheese) I. Title.
    SF271.S65 2005
    637'.35—dc22   2005017815
                                                       CIP

ISBN 1-59253-197-0

10 9 8 7 6 5 4 3

Design: Carol Petro
Cover Image: Allan Penn Photography

Printed in Singapore

To my patient wife Sharon, my joyful daughter Raya, and all of the friends and family who gave me support and encouragement throughout this project.

A special thanks goes out to my photographer, Allan Penn—a man who possesses a keen eye and a wicked sense of humor.

CONTENTS

INTRODUCTION

If you were to ask me when I received my college diploma what I would choose as a career, "cheese" would certainly have not been the answer. Like the vast majority of Americans, I had a limited exposure, at best, to cheese. Growing up, cheese consisted of American cheese, Parmesan in a green shaker, Cheese Wiz (sad but true), cream cheese, and an occasional assortment of Gouda chunks. Suffice it to say that appreciating cheese, let alone making it, were not activities I was familiar with. I fell into the discovery of this wondrous food by happy accident.

In the early 1990s, I was a substitute teacher of high school history in Boston, earning fifty dollars per day. Seeing that this was not enough to live on, I started working for the natural food retailer Bread & Circus, which was purchased by Whole Foods in the mid-1990s. I eventually managed the cheese department in one of the stores, and it was there that my transformation began.

It is possible that one taste of the complex, hauntingly tangy flavor of the goat cheese called chèvre could convert a cheese neophyte into an aficionado.

In short, I discovered that to learn to truly understand cheese was the perfect venue for a liberal arts major.

Those processed, soft cheeses fondly remembered from childhood, such as American cheese, Velveeta, and La Vache qui Rit (Laughing Cow), are sometimes the guilty pleasures of adults as well.

Although I wish I could say that all it took was one bite of a goat chèvre for me to be converted into a cheese fanatic, it was a gradual process. As I ate and read about seemingly strange and unique cheeses, I became hooked. If it wasn't the flavor that intrigued me, it was the history behind the cheese. If it wasn't the history, then it was the chemistry involved in making the cheese. If it wasn't the chemistry, then it was the biology behind the type of animal milk used to make the cheese. And if it wasn't the biology, then it was the linguistic history of the name of a particular cheese. In short, I discovered that to learn to truly understand cheese was the perfect venue for a liberal arts major.

Why Make Cheese

With so many cheeses becoming increasingly available to the average consumer, you might find yourself asking the question, "Why create cheeses at home?" To this I offer three simple answers: quality, savings, and self-satisfaction.

How many times have you purchased a Cheddar from your local supermarket and found the flavor to be less than exciting? Or an imported Gouda that had more flavor in the wax coating than in the cheese itself? Although many exceptional cheeses are imported into this country every week, they are, by far, the minority of what is available to the average person. By making your own cheese, you can create your own special variety or flavor of unbeatable quality.

A delectable cheese, such as this homemade blue cheese, can outclass its commercial equivalent in flavor, savings, and personal pride easily.

In terms of savings, making your own cheese has considerable cost advantages. Take something as commonplace as yogurt. When made by the quart at home, your yogurt costs 25 percent less than a quart of store-bought yogurt. Add to that the fact that you can blend as many flavorings into your homemade yogurt as you want, and you'll be better off than your local grocer.

Finally, you'll find tremendous satisfaction in making your own cheese. In a world where most of us are completely removed from the process of making most foods, making your own cheese will give you a greater understanding of its unique complexities. I assure you that once you have made your own Cheddar, you will never look at store-bought Cheddar the same way ever again.

PART ONE

How Tradition Influences Modern Cheese

*"Behind every piece
of cheese lies a little bit
of earth and sky."*

—ITALO CALVINO

Good cheeses have extraordinary eye appeal. They can be recognized by rich, creamy colors; interesting textures; and distinctive fragrances as well as memorable flavors.

CHAPTER ONE

A Brief History of Cheese Making

Cheese is one of the oldest foods known to humankind. Its origins and history often mirror the cultures, people, technology, and politics of the era during which it evolved. Quite simply, cheese is a reflection of what kind of people we are—our taste preferences and the kind of milk available to us for making cheese.

Ancient Origins

Cheese first came into existence about 8,000 years ago, when animals were domesticated. Archeological digs determined that cheese was made from both cows and goats in the Fertile Crescent—the area between the Tigris and Euphrates Rivers in modern-day Iraq. Other evidence includes a Sumerian frieze of milk animals and remnants of a material in the Tomb of Horus-Aha (3000 BC), which on analysis, proved to be cheese. Earthen cheese-making pots were also found in Egypt.

The centuries-old methods of cheese making have influenced how modern cheese looks and tastes, and for the hobbyist, the methods are little changed.

It is safe to assume that cheese went where the Romans went, along with their amphitheaters and aqueducts.

Artisan Advice Cheese is both ancient and important: It has been found in Egyptian tombs and was also used by the Greeks and Romans as currency to barter for goods.

As for written records, there are references to cheese in the Bible. Job cries out in frustration, "Hast thou not poured me out as milk, and curdled me like cheese?" (Job X). In the book of Samuel, this quote casts cheese in a more positive light: "Carry these ten cheeses to the captain of their thousand, and…bring back news of them" (Samuel XVII).

Other historical references to cheese are scarce until the time of the Greek and Roman Empires. One frequently cited example is from the *Odyssey* (Homer, 1184 BC), where a passage references cheese being made in the cave of the Cyclops. It is often speculated that this cheese is an early form of Feta, the cheese that is so closely associated with Greece.

The Roman Empire is often given credit for having a profound effect on the production and use of cheese as it spread its ideas and technology throughout its conquered lands. Along with amphitheaters and aqueducts, though not nearly as glamorous, it is safe to assume that cheese went where the Romans went. Cheese was so crucial to the Roman diet that the Emperor Diocletian (284–305 AD) set a maximum price for cheese, in an obvious attempt to curtail supply and price problems. A commonly cited mention of cheese was made by the Roman encyclopedist Pliny the Elder (23–89 AD), in his descriptions of the manufacture and uses of cheese.

It is impossible to know exactly what types of cheeses were made during ancient times, but one can certainly speculate. In this Mediterranean area of the world, with its temperate to hot climate, and lack of any natural refrigeration (such as caves), it is safe to assume that most of the cheeses were fresh and meant to be consumed soon after making.

The Middle Ages

Whereas Rome played a crucial role in advancing the widespread popularity of cheeses, so did Christianity—first through the spread of ideas and new food discoveries during the time of the Crusades, and then through actual pilgrimages to the Holy Land. But second, and most important to the art of cheese making, was the development of production technologies and cheese varieties in the monasteries and feudal states of Europe. Although the monastic movement played a significant role in the spread of Christianity, it also acted as a repository for knowledge. The monasteries played a crucial role in the advancement of agriculture and development of agricultural products in Europe: The best examples are wines, beer, and of course, cheese. As monks and nuns traveled throughout the communities from one nunnery or monastery to another, they undoubtedly brought with them the techniques of cheese making. It is interesting to note that there are types of cheese still produced today that were originally developed in monasteries. Some examples include Maroilles (from the Abbey of Maroilles in Avesnes, France), Port du Salut (from the Monastery of Notre Dame du Port du Salut in Laval, France), and Wenslydale (from the Rievaulx Abbey in Yorkshire, England).

During the Middle Ages, the feudal states throughout Europe were similar to the monasteries in that they were essentially closed communities. Lacking an efficient transportation system, residents were forced to rely on their own production of food. Within these states, people acquired specific agriculture-based skills, such as beer making, animal husbandry, and of course, cheese making. Their techniques for preserving milk as cheese were taught to future generations, thus creating regional specialties of cheese made from milk and flavoring

➤ Name-Protected Cheeses

Cheese has been a part of man's diet dating back to some of the earliest civilizations. It is interesting to note that some specific cheeses have quite an interesting history of their own. Documented references to Gorgonzola, for example, date back to 879 AD; Roquefort to 1070 AD; and Emmental to 50 BC. Although this is indeed impressive, it created a problem in the industrial age, starting at the turn of the twentieth century when cheese makers would call any blue cheese Gorgonzola because they knew it would sell better.

In an effort to preserve the integrity of foods, including cheese, the Stresa Convention was created in 1951, and ratified by France, Italy, Switzerland, Austria, Scandinavia, and the Netherlands. It was from this agreement that the appellations were formed. It is interesting to note that the United States was not a signatory to the agreement, which is why cheeses, such as Parmesan, Gorgonzola, and Romano, and wines, such as Champagne, could be produced under those names for many years without rebuke from the European countries. Although this agreement is still observed, there continue to be U.S. producers of the above cheeses and wine.

Many cheeses of European origin gained their names from the towns where they were first made, such as the creamy, velvet-textured Brie, which was named for the French town of Brie de Meaux.

What's in a Name?

When you consider the names of particular cheeses, you can often discover the regions of the world where they were developed. In some instances, they are named for a particular geographic region, such as Emmental, which is a valley in Switzerland, or for a town name, as in Brie de Meaux (the town of Meaux is 12½ miles [20 km] outside of Paris).

Other names come from vernacular language. Raclette is derived from the French word *racle*, which means "to scrape." A round of Raclette was traditionally cut in half and heated in front of a fire. The melted layers of cheese were then scraped onto food, such as boiled potatoes accompanied by cornichons (tiny tart pickles). As for Reblochon, this name is derived from the French word *reblocher*, meaning "to milk again."

Some cheese names go from the sublime to the ridiculous. Roquefort literally means "strong rock," in reference to the limestone caves in Calambou, France, where the famous cheese is aged to this very day. The goat cheese Crottin's name is derived from the word for "horse droppings," aluding to its unique shape.

indigenous to that particular region. Many of these particularities are found in cheeses today—they are called name-protected cheeses, carrying the designations of AOC (Appellation d'Origine Contrôllée) for France, DOP or DOC for Italy (Controlled designation of Origin), and DO (Denomination of Origin) or PDO (Protected Designation of Origin) for Spain.

Colonization

Cheese making came to North America via colonization in the 1600s. The regional differences reflected by the landscapes, animals, and cultures of the immigrants scattered across the continent influenced the kinds of cheeses made in early America. Immigrants were predominately British during the early stages of colonization, particularly in the Northeast United States. Even today, Cheddar remains the cheese

It is generally agreed that the first cheese factory established in the United States was in 1851 in Oneida County, New York, by a farmer named Jesse Williams. The "factory" was simply his farm. He had a reputation for making exceptional cheese, so his neighbors would send him their milk so that he could make cheese for them. This first effort was followed by a group of Wisconsin dairy farmers who started a Limburger factory in 1868. Even today the quality of Limburger from Wisconsin is equal to that found in Europe.

of choice in regards to consumption and production. Both New York State and Vermont are recognized for their production of Cheddars. It is also interesting to note that the first cheese factory in the United States was a Cheddar factory established in New York.

In the upper Midwest, immigrants were predominately German, Swiss, and Scandinavian, and the cheeses that continue to be produced there reflect that heritage. Wisconsin, which is a major cheese-producing state, makes a number of Emmentals. This type of cheese remains a staple for consumers throughout the region.

However, the immigrant cheese experience was not limited to the United States. In Canada, the cheese types reflect the country's bicultural heritage. Canadian Cheddar is well known, and Quebec produces a number of cheeses that reflect French traditions. Perhaps the best known of these is Oka, a washed-rind cheese that traces its roots to a Canadian monastery from the town with the same name. Oka is often compared to the French Port du Salut. Even in Argentina, where a large influx of Italian immigrants arrived during the 1920s, a cheese culture developed. Two of the major cheeses produced in that country are Reggianito, a take on the Italian Parmigiano Reggiano, and Provoletta, a version of provolone.

The Industrial Revolution

At the turn of the twentieth century, the Industrial Revolution brought a dramatic change to life in the Western world. With the creation of large factories, much of the rural population shifted to cities, having a dramatic effect on many aspects of life—including cheese making.

Until this time, cheese making was always a craft practiced on a small scale in local communities. Large-scale production created a number of problems for the cheese maker, the first one having to do with milk. In the past when cheese makers wanted milk for making cheese, they simply used milk from their own animals or those of a neighbor. But with the introduction of factories, the demand for milk quickly outstripped the local supply, which forced factories to find additional sources further away from the factory. Consequently, producers began pasteurizing their milk as a necessary sanitary precaution to assure cheese quality and safety for the extended trip from cow to factory. (For more on pasteurizing, see page 30.)

Another issue was the loss of regional variations of cheeses. In the pre-industrial age, cheese was a regional food with flavors that reflected the uniqueness of the local environment. As the seasons and grazing conditions changed, so too would the cheese. This was an accepted fact, and it was not seen as a flaw. But in factories, the emphasis was on profitability and consistency, and the quality of cheese suffered. One common complaint about modern cheese is that it is often boring and bland. That is not to say that all industrial cheeses are of poor quality and all small producers are exceptional, but cheeses produced in factories do tend to lack the certain effervescence that is often found in artisan cheeses.

The Rebirth of Artisan Cheese Making

So where do we stand today? Fueled by the communication revolution and the ease of international travel, people are exposed to and have developed a taste for the small artisan cheeses that have always been a part of Europe. Organizations such as the American Cheese Society in the United States and the Specialist Cheese Makers Association in the United Kingdom are helping to foster the development of small-production farmers and to introduce new varieties of cheeses. For the home cheese-making enthusiast, this could not be a better time to learn about cheese making.

The Festival of Cheeses: A Cheese Lover's Paradise

If you want to have a mind-blowing cheese experience, mark your calendar for the American Cheese Society's Festival of Cheeses. The festival is the capstone of the society's annual conference, and features hundreds of artisan and specialty cheeses created and presented by cheese professionals. It's not hard to see why it is such a popular event for cheese lovers. Where else can you see and taste so many varieties under one roof? The only word of warning for planning to attend the festival: come on an empty stomach.

CHAPTER TWO

Cheese-Making Basics

It is safe to say that practically everyone has begun the process of making cheese at one time or another, usually unintentionally. If you've had a bottle of spoiled milk sitting in the back of the refrigerator with the solids settled to the bottom, then you have the makings of what could become cheese. This curdled milk, with its sour flavor, has, shall we say, limited appeal as a cheese, but it does underscore the basic notion that cheese in its most essential element is simply soured milk. A cheese maker applies this principle in a controlled environment to provide a consistent product in a shorter period of time. This is accomplished by adding a combination of cultures and enzymes to milk. And because milk is the base for cheese, it is best to start by looking at the composition of milk, learning what types of milk can be used for cheese making, and discovering some of the unique influences various kinds of milk can have on cheese quality.

Milk is the base for all cheeses, so the logical place to begin, for a first-time cheese maker, is looking at the composition of milk, learning what types of milk can be used for cheese making, and discovering some of the unique influences on the quality of various cheeses that can be attributed to the milk used to make them.

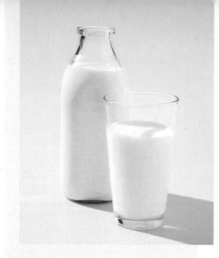

The essence of exceptional cheese lies in the quality of the milk used to make it.

Composition of Milk

The average person likely does not give milk a second thought. It's there at every supermarket and convenience store, readily available in every container size and flavor imaginable. In a sense, we take milk for granted. To a cheese maker, however, milk is something glorious—it's a gift from Mother Nature and from a generous animal. If you were to ask any artisan cheese maker about the milk he or she uses to make cheese, he or she will wax on eloquently about its composition, the animal source, and its general characteristics. So let's look into this subject a little further.

Milk is often called nature's most perfect food, because it supplies almost all of the nutrients and vitamins that the human body requires (the notable exceptions are vitamin C and iron). This nutritious drink has been a mainstay of mankind for countless centuries, and for nearly as long, man has been using it as the main ingredient for cheese. Milk is composed of several major components. Four of these components—fat, casein, lactose, and whey protein—are essential to properly making cheese.

FAT Fat plays a crucial role in cheese production. It is one of the main components responsible for flavor and aroma. It also plays a key role in forming the texture and body of a cheese, particularly in the ripened cheeses, such as Camembert or Alsatian Muenster. As anyone who has tasted a low-fat cheese knows, it lacks flavor and texture—quite simply, it doesn't taste like cheese. Although fat can be a loaded word in today's world, it is an essential element for making cheese.

Creamy, soft-textured, rich-tasting cheeses such as Camembert owe their melt-in-the-mouth goodness to high milk-fat content.

The delectably stringy quality of some types of cheese, such as mozzarella—the crowning glory of pizza—comes from an elastic component of milk that is called casein.

CASEIN Casein is the major protein found in milk. Casein is suspended in milk, meaning that it does not dissolve. This is an important distinction, because it makes casein available for extraction by a chemical process, which ultimately leads to the creation of cheese. Casein, because of its unique structure, has elastic qualities that can shrink or expand, giving cheese its elastic texture. Quite simply, casein combined with fats make up most of the raw material needed to make cheese.

WHEY PROTEIN Whey protein comprises only 0.6% of milk. Unlike casein, which is suspended in milk and provides the majority of protein, whey protein is soluble in milk, meaning it is contained within the liquid. Consequently, whey protein retains more moisture than casein and is nonelastic. For these reasons, it is a secondary source of solids for making cheese, traditionally ricotta.

LACTOSE Lactose is milk sugar, or more correctly, a carbohydrate. It is an essential element to cheese making because it provides the necessary energy for the beneficial bacteria in milk to grow and thrive, thereby starting the fermentation process. Without lactose, there would be no cheese.

Types of Animal Milk and Their Influence on Cheese

Although a cheese can, in theory, be made from any lactating animal (historical references in ancient Rome cite cheese made with mare's milk), the vast majority of the world's cheeses come from one of three animals: cow, goat, or sheep. All milks contain the aforementioned elements, but there are differences between the various breeds of each species of animal that have a profound effect on any cheese made from it.

Whey is a protein-rich, watery by-product of making cheese and yogurt. It can be used in baking or to make other cheeses, such as Ricotta and Gjetost.

The Importance of Cleanliness

Cheese is created by specific bacteria and other organisms, and cross contamination from other kinds of bacteria found in your kitchen can spoil a batch of cheese. Bacteria can keep cheese from setting up properly, give it a bitter or off flavor, or worse—make it unhealthy to eat.

Choose glass, stainless-steel, or food-grade plastic equipment that can be sterilized. Avoid porous materials, such as disposable plastics and wooden utensils, which are difficult to sterilize.

Before making cheese, sterilize all of your equipment. To sterilize your milk-heating pan, pour water into the pan to a depth of about 2" (5 cm). Set the lid on the pan, and boil the water for ten minutes. Drain the water before adding the milk.

Keep a pan of water at a rolling boil, and put your cheese cloth, mats, knives, stirring spoons, curd knife, and other utensils into the water for a minimum of five minutes (or leave them in until you are ready to use them). Pans, molds, colanders, and other larger pieces of equipment can be adequately cleaned by running them through the dishwasher right before using them.

Jersey cows are considered by many artisans to be the best breed for cheese making due to the high butterfat content of their milk.

Cow's milk cheeses are flavorful, with a creamy consistency that varies depending on the cream content of the milk.

Goat's milk cheeses have a creamy consistency and a tangier flavor than cheeses made from cow's milk.

Cow's Milk

In the Western world, the vast majority of cheeses produced and consumed are made with cow's milk. This is primarily due to historical influences (cows were brought over on the boats for the settlement of the Jamestown colony in 1606), and the fact that the climate and terrain are suitable to their nature. Cows require large tracts of land, abundant vegetation, and temperate climates, all of which exist in North America. Their milk is rich and creamy, with high moisture content and large fat globules that rise to the surface. These qualities, combined with a firm casein structure, make it easy to use for cheese making. It is important to also remember that there are variations in milk quality within the different breeds of cattle. Holsteins, the most popular breed for producing drinking milk, make milk with a fat content of 3.5–4%, whereas the creamy milk of Jersey cows—which are preferred by cheese makers—tops out at 5.4%.

Goat's Milk

Although goat's milk cheeses are a relatively recent phenomenon in the United States, they are very common in many parts of the world. Goats are hardy creatures that can survive in extreme climates with scant, poor-quality vegetation for food. Unlike cows, which have a specific diet, goats will eat a varied diet with little fanfare. Goat's milk is partially homogenized (meaning that it contains small fat particles held in suspension in the milk), although there is some cream separa-

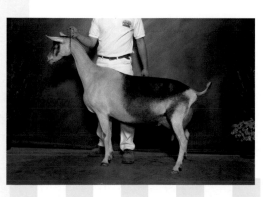

The Swiss Alpine breed of goats, such as the 2002 Grand Champion show winner shown here, is the most popular variety of goat for cheese makers due to its generous milk production.

tion. It also has smaller fat globules compared to those of cow's milk. Consequently, goat's milk cheeses have a smoother, softer texture than cow's milk cheeses. Goat cheeses have a distinctive tangy, some even say gamey, flavor.

Sheep's Milk

Sheep are sturdy animals that can live in areas that no cow would dare consider. Because of their thick, wooly coats, they can survive in some of the harshest conditions. It is for this reason that sheep's milk cheeses tend to come from the more challenging regions of the world—windy, rocky climates with little vegetation. Think of the arid regions of Greece or Sicily, and you will get the idea. Sheep's milk is an amazing product. Fully homogenized, it is the densest of the three milks. It is interesting to note that whereas a cow will produce considerably more milk compared to a sheep (ten gallons versus one quart per day), the amount of solids is almost identical. Sheep's milk cheeses are dense with oil and butterfat, which come to the surface of the cheese, making for a rich and flavorful product. Although some of the world's great cheeses are made from sheep's milk, there are few, if any, sheep dairies in the United States. This prized commodity is a tough find for the home cheese maker (see Resources, page 173).

Sheep's milk cheeses—and sheep's milk itself—although flavorful and creamy, are harder to find than cow's and goat's milk and cheeses, because sheep produce less milk. A breed native to Germany, East Frisian sheep, shown here, are preferred for their comparatively high milk production.

✦ Artisan Advice In spite of the fact that they produce only about a quart (or liter) of milk a day, sheep were the first animals milked by people. Sheep were milked 3,000 years before cows.

This pepper jack was derailed because the curds were not pressed at a sufficient pressure for them to set properly. If your cheese is pressed properly, and it still refuses to set, then immerse the cheese in 100°F (38°C) water for one minute, then press for thirty minutes, to encourage the process.

What Can Go Wrong

When it comes to making cheese, moderation is the key, beginning with warming the milk. Whether you are pasteurizing raw milk or warming pasteurized milk to prepare it for making cheese, do so very slowly. Keep a thermometer in the pan and consult it often. If you heat the milk too quickly, the rapid increase in temperature will kill the helpful bacteria and enzymes that convert the milk to cheese.

How Grazing, Season, and Geography Affect Milk

Whatever an animal eats will have a direct effect on the quality of its milk, which in turn affects the quality of the cheese made from it. So in addition to the breed and the type of animal, a cheese maker must continually consider the external factors that will affect the diet of the animal.

Take grazing as an example. A cow fed a diet rich in fresh, wild grasses will produce richer, more flavorful milk. The milk from animals that graze on wild grasses contains lower cholesterol and higher omega-3 acid ratings than the milk of their penned, silage-fed kin—proof that a happy grazer is a healthy grazer. Conversely, if the cow is fed dried, stale grasses and fermented silage, the flavor of the milk will suffer, as will the cheese.

The time of year also plays an important role in cheese making. Winter is not considered the ideal season for cheese making, especially in cold climates where cows must eat silage. Where animals graze also comes into play. If cows are situated in a coastal region, it is more than likely that the milk, and consequently the cheese, will have a salty note due to the salt that sea breezes deposit on the grasses.

All of these influences can best be summoned up by the French word *terroir*. Most dictionaries translate this word as "soil" or "country," which is not entirely accurate. Terroir can best be described as the soul of a particular spot on earth. A particular terroir can be arid or damp, mountainous or flat, cold or hot—each terroir is unique. This is one explanation for the different characteristic flavors of many regional cheeses.

A cow that has a diet rich in fresh, wild grasses will produce richer, more flavorful milk.

Artisan Advice Cows milked in the evening give milk that's higher in fat content and better for making cheese than milk extracted in the morning.

Raw milk is revered among cheese makers because of the complex and delicious flavorings it brings to cheese made from it, but it must be collected under sanitary conditions to prevent possible pathogens from entering the cheese.

Forms of Milk

Milk comes in many different forms; some are suitable for cheese making, and others, not so well suited. Here is a quick summary.

Raw Milk

In the cheese-making world, raw or unpasteurized milk is seen as the gold standard. The reason for this is that raw milk contains all of the microflora and enzymes that the animal has ingested from grazing in its own unique terroir. In essence, it could be said that raw-milk cheeses are the direct descendants of the cheese makers of antiquity. Questions are often raised about food safety and raw milk, but it is generally agreed that raw milk is safe to consume if it is kept clean. Indeed, if any foreign microorganism is introduced into the milk, it would have a noticeable negative consequence on the resulting cheese, taking the form of bloating, off flavors, and off aromas.

If raw-milk cheeses are your preference, it is best to buy your raw milk from a known and trusted source. The regulations regarding the buying and selling of raw milk vary by state and are tightly controlled. A specific listing can be found in the Resources section of this book (see page 172).

Most forms of milk, including everything from raw to pasteurized milk, homogenized and even nonfat powdered dry milk, are acceptable for making select cheeses. The notable exception is Ultra Heat-Treated milk (UHT), which is packaged in sealed boxes and stocked on grocery shelves at room temperature.

Terroir can best be described as the soul of a particular spot on earth. Each terroir is unique, and is one explanation for the different characteristic flavors of regional cheeses.

Food Safety and Raw Milk Cheeses

Is it safe to make and eat raw-milk cheese? This is question that continually comes up, so let's look at a few of the major points.

■ Is pasteurized milk safer to use than raw milk? Any milk whether raw or pasteurized has a relatively neutral pH, which makes it a perfect host for pathogenic bacteria. Pasteurization will assure that the milk you use is free of any pathogen *before* you use it. If your equipment is not sterilized, however, your cheese could be open to contamination from a pathogen. The bottom line is that no milk is absolutely safe; there is always potential for problems with either raw or pasteurized milk.

■ Are all pasteurized cheeses safer than raw milk cheeses? Not necessarily. Fresh cheeses and soft-ripened cheeses, because of their high moisture content and high pH, could pose potential problems for food safety whether they are pasteurized or not. Aged cheeses, any cheeses that are aged over sixty days, are safe, whether they're made with raw milk or pasteurized.

The most important thing to remember in all of this is that cheese is a stable food that poses little health risk as long as the basic rules of sanitation are followed.

At the time this book is being written, raw milk is legally sold in the United States in twenty-eight out of fifty states. In an additional five states, raw milk can be sold for animal consumption, under which one could imply that humans are animals. The other option to explore is a cow-share program. This is a system in which a group of consumers pay a farmer a fee for boarding, feeding, and milking their cows (or share of a cow). The cow-share owner then obtains, but does not purchase, milk from his or her own cow. Think of this as a time share in the bovine world (without the telemarketers), and you get the idea.

The advantage of raw milk: *It's a full-flavored milk that produces rich-flavored cheeses.*

The disadvantage of raw milk: *Raw milk is not easy to find, and in some areas may be impossible to find.*

Pasteurized Milk

Pasteurization is the process of heat-treating milk as a way of killing off any potentially harmful bacteria or pathogens that could be in the milk. Before World War II, there were virtually no cheeses made from pasteurized milk. Pasteurization became a necessity for two reasons. First, the long-distance transportation of milk to cheese factories made contamination a possibility. Second, milk from a variety of places could lead to variances in the milk flavor, which would ultimately lead to differences in flavor of the cheese produced. A cheese could potentially taste different depending on the source of milk in each batch. For the small cheese maker, this variation could be considered normal. For the larger producer, where consistency is the key to success, it could lead to disaster. To avoid inconsistency, the factories used pasteurization as one of several methods to assure that milk had, and still has, a consistent flavor profile.

There are two methods of pasteurization. The standard method used by the majority of commercial cheese makers and virtually all dairy companies, is called High Temperature Short Hold, or HTSH. Using this method, milk is heated to 158°F to 162°F (70°C–72°C) for fifteen seconds and then rapidly cooled down to a stable 45°F to 55°F (7°C–13°C). HTSH presents one major problem. The high heat kills virtually all bacteria in the milk—both helpful and potentially harmful. For this reason, it is necessary to introduce bacteria strains into HTSH-pasteurized milk when making cheese. The added bacteria will bring flavor to the cheese but cannot replicate the complexities that nature provides in raw milk.

An alternative form of pasteurization, which is called Low Temperature Long Hold, or LTLH, uses less heat (135°F to 155°F [58°C–68°C]) but a longer time, holding the milk at the maximum temperature for a full thirty minutes. For an artisan cheese maker, LTLH is the preferred method of pasteurization because some flavor-enhancing enzymes and bacteria will survive the process. Another major issue with HTST-pasteurization is that it destroys all of the enzymes found in milk, one of them being lactase, which helps in aiding the digestion of milk. (See sidebar, "A Word on Lactose Intolerance," page 33.)

The advantages of pasteurized milk: *It is readily available virtually everywhere, and the supply of this milk is consistent.*

The disadvantages of pasteurized milk: *You will need to add calcium chloride during cheese making if the milk is homogenized. The milk is usually HTSH pasteurized, so it will have fewer enzymes, giving the milk a flatter taste.*

⇒ Pasteurizing Your Milk at Home

The issue regarding pasteurized milk and cheese can get quite emotional at times. But the most important thing to remember is that we are all looking to safely produce good and flavorful cheeses. If you follow the general sanitation principals and use common sense you should be fine. In terms of your milk source, if you have access to raw milk and have concerns about the soundness of the milk, then by all means pasteurize. The easiest way to do it follows:

1. Place the milk in a sterilized double boiler, and gradually raise the temperature to 145°F (66°C). Stir often so that the heat is distributed evenly. Keep the milk at a consistent temperature for thirty minutes. If you find that the temperature has dropped below the target point, you will have to raise the level and start the timing over again.

2. At the end of thirty minutes, rapidly cool the milk. The most effective way of doing this is to set the milk pan into an ice-water bath. Do not use straight ice because it will not cool the milk fast enough. Again, stir frequently to ensure even cooling.

3. Store in a clean, sanitized container in the refrigerator. The milk will last for two weeks.

Homogenized Milk

Homogenization is the process of breaking down the fat globules in milk to a size smaller than two micrometers. At that size, the forces of gravity do not affect the cells, so the cream will not rise to the surface of the milk. (Non-homogenized milk is also known as "cream-line" milk and is instantly recognizable by the thick layer of cream that settles at the top of the bottle.)

Homogenization is done by forcing milk through a series of small-gauge pipes at high pressure, which causes shearing of the fat globules. For a cheese maker, homogenized milk does present a problem in that the curd structure is softer and does not coagulate as easily as it does in milk that has not been homogenized. Nonetheless, it can be used for all cheese making, through the use of additional rennet and calcium chloride, a salt that absorbs moisture and aids in the development of the curds.

The advantages of homogenized milk: *It can be found everywhere and is suitable for virtually all cheese recipes.*

The disadvantage of homogenized milk: *It requires the addition of calcium chloride in order to form curds properly.*

Powdered Milk

Although it may sound a bit sacrilegious, you can make cheese from powdered milk. Because it is a low-fat product, you are limited to the types of cheeses you can make, primarily fresh cheeses such as quark or cottage cheese. But if you are in a pinch, drag out a box of good old powdered milk and go for it!

The advantage of powdered milk: *Convenience—you can keep it on the pantry shelf.*

The disadvantage of powdered milk: *Only a limited number of cheeses can be produced with it.*

Artisan Advice Milk taken late in a cow's lactating cycle has a higher fat and protein content, making it better suited to producing cheese than milk taken soon after calving. Milk taken early in the lactating cycle contains colostrums, which prevent proper cheese formation.

UHT Milk

Ultra Heat-Treated (UHT) milk is popular in other parts of the world, but in the United States it barely makes a showing in the total consumer milk market. UHT milk has been treated at a whopping 275°F to 300°F (135°C–150°C). Ouch! Its popularity lies in the fact that it does not require refrigeration until after the package has been opened, thus giving it an extended shelf life. Walk into a French supermarket, and you will be amazed at the UHT milk displays sitting outside of refrigeration. Needless to say, this is a sterile product that cannot be used for cheese making.

Bottom line: *Not suitable for cheese making.*

Cultures and Rennet: The Other Pieces of the Puzzle

All cheese making is based on the coagulation of milk solids into a curd mass. There are essentially two ways to accomplish this, depending on what your recipe calls for—with an acid or with rennet. Rennet is an enzyme that coagulates milk and causes the curds to form (for more on curd formation, see page 83). In the case of an acid coagulation, the procedure is simple. An acid, typically in the form of lemon juice or vinegar, is added to heated milk, allowing the curd mass to form. With a rennet cheese, the milk must have the proper acidity for the rennet to be effective, and this requires using a starter culture.

A Word on Lactose Intolerance

Mentioning lactose intolerance is enough to produce a pall over the brow of any committed cheese lover. This malady is a result of the body's inability to produce enough of the lactase enzyme to enable it to digest milk. Virtually all infants produce lactase, but this ability diminishes by the age of four. And whereas all other mammals stop producing the enzyme, most adult humans are unique in that they still produce the enzyme in small quantities. Lactase is naturally occurring in unpasteurized milk, but it does not survive the heating that takes place during pasteurization.

So what are the options for the cheese lover with this affliction? You have three choices. First, start off with hard, aged cheeses. The majority of lactose is found in the whey, and harder cheeses have considerably less whey than softer cheeses. If softer cheeses are your desire, you may want to try goat's-milk cheeses, because they are naturally lower in lactic acid, or try yogurt cheese, because yogurt contains bacteria that assist in the digestion of milk. Finally, you can reintroduce lactase into your cheeses with some of the popular digestive aides, such as LactAid and Lactase. Simply add it to your milk, as directed on the package, and let the milk sit refrigerated for twenty-four hours before you make your cheese. You may notice that the milk tastes slightly sweeter after treating, but no major change occurs in the milk.

Starter Cultures

A starter culture, as the name implies, is a mixture of milk bacteria that is added to milk with the distinct purpose of making it more acidic. As the bacteria consume the lactose, they produce a by-product called lactic acid. The longer the cultures thrive, the more acid they produce, the more soured the milk becomes, and the easier it is to contract the size of the curds, which will then expel more whey. This step is essential, because the more whey that is removed from the milk, the more the curd particles will be assisted in combining to form cheese.

The acidity will also affect the flavor of the cheese. Although it is obvious that overly acidic milk will result in a sour cheese, the same can be said for under-acidified milk. In the case of the latter, the curds will retain excessive amounts of whey, giving the cheese a puckerish flavor.

There are two types of starter cultures: mesophilic and thermophilic. Mesophilic cultures are moderate-temperature bacteria used when the curds are not going to be heated to higher than 102°F (30°C). Mesophilic cultures are typically used for Cheddars, Goudas, and other hard cheeses. Thermophilic cultures are heartier bacteria that can survive up to 132°F (55°C). They are used for making Swiss-style cheeses and the harder Italian cheeses, such as Parmesan and Romano. In addition to acidifying milk, these starter cultures play a key role in the flavor development of the harder cheeses.

Starter cultures come in two formats, a mother culture and a direct set. Both of these are available from the cheese making supply companies listed in the Resources section of this book (see page 172).

see page 172

Artisan Advice Starter cultures from a cheese-making supplier are a blend of various forms of lactocci, lactobacilli, and streptococci, combined to produce a specific flavor profile. But suppose you want to get started making your cheese right away and don't want to wait for a shipment from the supplier. All you have to do is go to your local supermarket and purchase some buttermilk or yogurt. The active cultures in buttermilk are the low-temperature mesophilic type, which can be used for making pressed uncooked cheeses. Yogurt contains the high-temperature thermophilic type useful in making Parmesan and Romano.

A mother culture for making cheese has a thickened yogurtlike consistency and is rich in the beneficial bacteria that turn milk into cheese. Mother cultures are an old-fashioned and authentic way to make cheese and, like sourdough starter cultures used for making bread, they can be kept going indefinitely.

Rennet

Rennet is used for making the vast majority of cheeses. Rennet is not necessary if enough acidity is present in the milk to cause it to coagulate, but rennet does speed up the process and form a stronger, tighter curd, a characteristic that makes rennet essential for many of the classic harder cheeses.

Rennet comes in two forms, an animal product and a vegetable product. Animal rennet comes from the fourth stomach of an unweaned calf, kid, or lamb. Within the young animal's stomach walls lies an enzyme called chymosin, which curdles the mother's milk, making it easier for the young animal to digest. For centuries, cheese makers would add small strips of stomach (which contained chymosin) to the batch of milk that they were working with, creating the first modern rennet.

Romans also used a variety of plants to coagulate the milk. Non-animal rennet, such as bark from the fig tree, was often used in ancient Rome. Today's vegetable rennet is based on a specific mold named *Muror miehei*. This mold contains *chymosin* and is identical in structure to the animal rennet.

Acidity

The level of acidity throughout the cheese-making process is a crucial component for the cheese maker. The amount of acidity has a major effect on the texture of the cheese. The higher the acidity, the more moisture retained by the curds and the softer the cheese, all things being equal. The acidity will also affect the flavor of the cheese, giving it sharp flavors.

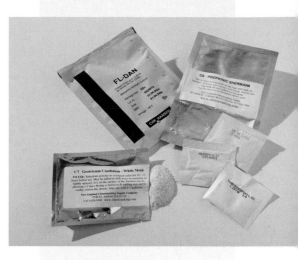

Rennet *and prepackaged starter cultures simplify cheese making and ensure even results* **for home cheese makers.**

*Rennet is as old as cheese making—
It is widely known that the Romans used
a variety of plants to coagulate milk.*

Acidity plays a crucial role in ripening the milk, because it is a by-product of the interaction of the starter cultures with lactose. In the easier cheese recipes, less attention needs to be paid to the acidity levels of the milk, but as you progress into making more difficult cheeses, you should be comfortable with monitoring acidity.

Molds and External Bacteria

Although the discussion until now has been focused on the starting process of making cheeses, let's take a quick look at one of the finishing processes, which has to do with molds and external bacteria. Molds are fungi, or the odd cousin of mushrooms. They are aerobic parasites requiring a host for survival; high-protein, high-moisture foods such as cheese are ideal. When applied to the surface of a cheese, these special molds will grow on the surface and slowly penetrate the interior of the cheese (for commercial sources for cheese molds, see Resources, page 172). As the mold makes its way toward the center of the cheese, the mold consumes the lactic acid in the milk (and gives off an ammonia smell), which helps to soften the fats and proteins. The process is affected by time, temperature, and humidity.

It is interesting to cut open a wheel of Brie that has not fully ripened to see the effects of the ripening process. Where the mold has not penetrated the cheese, there is a hard, dense "bar" running through the center of the cheese. If you taste this area you'll notice that the cheese has a decidedly sour note and the texture is dry and crumbly. The same holds true for blue cheese. A young blue that has

⇒ The pH Scale

The pH scale is used to determine the concentration of hydrogen ions, which indicate the level of acidity or alkalinity in any given compound. The scale's range starts at zero and ends at fourteen. Water, with a pH of seven, is considered neutral. Anything with a pH rating below seven is acidic, and anything above is considered alkaline. So, a lower pH means a higher acidity. In the cheese world, milk has a pH of 6.6 (you may notice a slight acid aftertaste when you drink a glass of milk). Cheddars have a final pH of 5.3, whereas fresh cheeses, such as quark or cottage cheese, have a pH of 4.5. (Just for comparison, vinegar has pH of 2.9.) It should not be surprising that fresh cheeses are more acidic, because they contain more lactic acid, which gives them that puckerish flavor.

When applied to the surface of a cheese, special strains of molds such as Penicillium roqueforti will grow on the surface and slowly penetrate the interior of the cheese, creating lovely blue veins and an earthy, mushroomlike flavor. Although often confused with medicinal Penicillin, this is a different strain of mold, and will not produce an adverse reaction in those who are allergic to the antibiotic.

not had much time to mature will be noticeably absent of the dramatic veining, and its flavor will also have more of the sour notes and less of the rich blue flavors that people love. For home cheese making, the following molds are typically used.

Penicillium candidum

This is the white mold that is often associated with Brie cheeses. Light and airy in appearance, it helps the cheese mature in flavor and texture as it works its way through the cheese. Without the mold, Brie would remain rubbery with a decidedly sour flavor.

Geotrichum candidum

This ripening mold is used in conjunction with *Penicillium candidum* or *Brevibacterium linens*. With soft-ripened cheeses it will have a positive effect on the flavor and appearance, and help to prevent the rind from slipping off the cheese. In the case of washed-rind cheeses, *G. candidum* will aid the growth of the *Brevibacterium linens*.

Penicillium roqueforti

Perhaps the most famous of cheese molds, *Penicillium roqueforti* is most often used for making blue cheese. Originally found in the Roquefort caves in Roquefort, France, it provides this cheese with its unique, robust, sometimes described as hot flavors.

The white, airy coating on cheeses such as Brie and Camembert is due to the addition of the mold Penicillium candidum.

⤳ Brie of a Different Color

Although we associate Brie cheese with its delicate white exterior, this is not the traditional appearance of the cheese. Because these cheeses were allowed to ripen in the open, they took on many different colors, including blue and brown. The use of *Penicillium candidum*, which produces a powdery white coating, was introduced in 1910, as a way to standardize the production of factory-made Brie cheeses.

Long after leaving his childhood home in the Pyrenees mountains between France and Spain, cheese maker Eran Wajswol still remembered the flavors of the creamy sheep's milk yogurt and cheese of his homeland. Eventually this mechanical engineer opened Farmersville Cheeses, New Jersey's only raw-milk cheese producer making cheese from sheep's milk—and it was a career change he never regretted.

As he explains, "A love of farming, the attachment to the soil and animals, and the challenging set of circumstances in farming may be one of the most fulfilling ways to live one's life. Cheese making adds another dimension, bringing together chemistry, science, and art. There are no 'for sures' in artisan cheese making. Each batch is a challenge; each great batch is a personal victory."

When comparing sheep's milk cheese to cow's milk cheese, Wajswol says, "Sheep's milk makes a solid curd that forms into a wheel of cheese almost by itself. At the end of the season, when the solids in the milk almost double, it is tough to get one's hand into the curd for stirring. You will not see this in cow's milk."

Wajswol has a piece of advice for home cheese makers who want to try aged, pressed cheeses: "Like every other step in the process, pressing cheese is a give-and-take game. You should press to remove whey, but you should not press too hard, or you will close the pores in the rind and trap the whey. Mistakes manifest themselves quickly into ugly rinds."

Brevibacterium linens

Used for cheeses known as surface-ripened or smear cheeses, *Brevibacterium linens* is a naturally occurring bacteria that, when applied to the surface of a cheese, will aid it in the ripening process, much along the lines of the previously mentioned molds. The bacterial smear is applied to the surface of the cheese where it develops into a series of colonies. As the cheese ripens, the surface must be washed, typically with a brine solution (but in some cases, beer, wine, or spirits), to distribute the colonies evenly over the surface. The ripening process for these cheeses depends on how intense a flavor the cheese maker wants. Usually, these cheeses are strong with an intense odor. That unmistakable smell is a result of the *Brevibacterium* releasing the sulfur gases in the milk as it ripens the cheese, giving the cheese a unique aroma. *B. linens* is most often associated with cheeses such as Limburger or Alsatian Muenster.

Other Ingredients

Vegetable Ash

Vegetable ash is used for ripened cheeses, most famously with goat cheeses. Ash was traditionally used by local cheese makers in France because it provides a natural coat that creates a friendly environment for surface-ripening molds to grow.

A wide assortment of fresh and dried herbs can add piquant flavor and color to cheeses.

Herbs and Other Flavorings

You can add many different things to your cheese to give it an extra flavor kick. The most obvious additions are the hot peppers found in cheeses, such as Monterey Jack, or the herbes de Provence found in fresh goat chèvre. You can experiment with almost any spice. Mustard seeds are a good choice for Gouda. Goat cheese logs rolled in paprika are very interesting and have a dynamic look. Whatever you choose, remember that with the softer cheeses, the herbs need to marry with the cheese to infuse it with flavor, so let the cheese sit for a day or two in the refrigerator.

The ripening process for these cheeses depends on how intense a flavor the cheese maker wants. The unmistakable smell is a result of the Brevibacterium linens.

Salt

Salt plays a multifaceted role in cheese making; it is an essential element that cannot be overlooked. Because salt restricts the growth of bacteria, it is used toward the end of the cheese-making process to slow down the growth of the lactic bacteria as well as to inhibit the growth of any foreign bacteria that might have gotten into the milk. In addition, salt acts as a dehydrator, drying out the cheese, thus making the curd structure smaller. Salt also adds flavor to cheese.

For cheese making, do not use basic table salt, as it typically contains iodine. It is necessary to use noniodized salt when making cheese, because iodine will retard or kill the growth of the starter cultures in the cheese. There are several types of salt you can use: kosher salt, canning salt, or cheese salt.

Ripening

The final stage of cheese making is the ripening. Ripening is associated with rennet-coagulated cheeses, which are typically matured for a period of three weeks to two years, depending on the type of cheese. After a cheese maker has followed a recipe and produced a raw product ready for maturation, it's time for the cheese to develop into something beautiful and tasty. The process of ripening is a complex relationship between the curds, salt, rennet, and culture.

Although there are suggested times for ripening a cheese, there is no hard-and-fast rule, because many different cheeses can be consumed at different stages of ripeness, depending on the flavor preference. The only exception to this would be with cheeses for which the flavor will be noticeably inferior if consumed when young, such as blue cheese. It is interesting to note that the length of aging is related inversely to the amount of moisture in the cheese. This is due to the fact that any cheese with high moisture content is susceptible to breakdown from the increased activity of the bacteria in the cheese.

The ripening process itself is a result of a series of complex biochemical reactions involving one or more of the following media:

- rennet
- naturally occurring enzymes found in the milk— especially important when making raw-milk cheeses
- starter culture and the enzymes found within it
- secondary microorganisms and the enzymes found within them

One example of a secondary microorganism is propionic acid, which is a bacterium that is added to Emmental cheese, giving it its unique holes, or "eye development," as we say in the business. Other examples of secondary microorganisms are the molds and bacteria used for ripening cheese that are explained in further detail below.

The process of ripening involves three biochemical changes: glycolysis, lipolysis, and proteolysis. Each one involves conversion by enzymes of a particular substance into simpler compounds (glycolysis involves sugars, lipolysis involves fats [that is, lipids], and proteolysis involves proteins). Simple compounds, such as peptides and short-chain fatty acids, are crucial in transmitting flavor.

Another thing to keep in mind is that as a cheese ages, it is slowly dehydrating. When a cheese loses moisture, the fats and proteins are concentrated. This in turn will give the cheese a fuller flavor and a creamier, denser texture. Granted, this explanation is an oversimplification of a very complicated process, but it helps to define some of the variables at work when making cheese.

The process is a complex relationship between the curds, salt, rennet, and culture. Many different cheeses can be consumed at different stages of ripeness, depending on the flavor preference.

PART TWO
Making Cheese

*"Cheese, wine, and a friend
must be old to be good."*

–CUBAN PROVERB

The process of making cheese, in many ways, can be just as fulfilling as eating it. Whether it is the fresh yogurt with which you top your fresh fruit or the section of cheddar that you cut from the wheel, the fruits of your labor will be ample reward for the time spent. With a few simple pieces of equipment, such as a cheese press, molds, and standard kitchen utensils, you are ready to make cheese.

CHAPTER THREE

Basic Cheese Making: Getting Started

The best place to start making cheese is with fresh cheeses. They are the easiest to make, require little special equipment, and do not demand any serious time commitment in terms of making or aging. Fresh cheeses are sometimes known as acid-curd cheeses, because in some cases they rely on acid alone (or acid in combination with heat) to create the coagulation of the curd. Depending on the type of cheese you make, you can start in the morning or early afternoon and, in a few hours, have cheese ready for your evening meal.

However, there are some drawbacks to fresh cheeses. They are very mild and have subtle flavors, although they can be spiced up with the addition of herbs, fruits, or vegetables. Fresh cheeses also have a short shelf life and need to be consumed rather quickly—in some cases, the same day that they are made. Although a two-year-old Cheddar makes people salivate, the same cannot be said of a two-year-old cream cheese, if you catch my drift.

Fresh cheeses, such as the Neufchâtel shown here, are a joy to make, because they can be made and eaten—fresh—the same day.

A Few Words on Sanitation

Before we commence with the cheese-making process, it is imperative to take a serious look at proper sanitation procedures. Although cheese as a food is generally safe to consume, it does have the potential to produce serious food illness, so it is best to follow basic sanitation procedures when making your own.

First, you must sterilize your equipment. There are several ways to do this.

One method is to simply put all of your utensils in boiling water for five minutes, and then let them air-dry. This is the best method for sterilizing your milk-heating pan and metal tools, such as slotted spoons, curd knives, and so on (for more information, see The Importance of Cleanliness, on page 25).

Alternatively, you can create a mild bleach solution using two tablespoons (28 ml) of household bleach to one gallon (3.8 L) of water. This solution works equally well for sterilizing tools. You want this to be a mild solution, so don't go overboard. Be sure to rinse off and air-dry all utensils, because any bleach residue will have an adverse effect on the cheese cultures and rennet. When you are finished making your cheese, thoroughly clean all of your tools in hot water and dish detergent, and store them in a clean place.

In all cases, remember to relax when it comes to sanitation. We're making cheese here, not running an operating room. Use common sense. Cheese has been made for more than 2,000 years, mostly with tools that today would not be considered safe by your local health department. If by chance your cheese becomes contaminated, you will more than likely run into a greater risk of hurting your cheese than you will of causing an illness.

In all cases, remember to relax— we're making cheese here, not running an operating room.

⇛ Equipment

For making the basic fresh cheeses, most of the equipment you'll need can be found in your kitchen.

Colander: Any type of colander will do, but I prefer one with a high-footed bottom, so the whey will not touch the cheese.

Slotted Spoon: Stainless steel is best.

Cooking Pot: Again, stainless steel is preferred. Cast-iron and aluminum should not be used, because they are reactive to acids and will give your cheese a metallic flavor. You may want to consider buying a pot designated for cheese making. This will spare you the frustration of having to scrub the burn stains off the bottom of your catch-all pasta pot before making cheese. In any case, be certain that your pot is large enough to accommodate two to three gallons of milk. There is nothing worse than starting off with a pot that's too small, and then scrambling to find a bigger one.

Cheese Cloth or Butter Muslin: The cheese cloth found in a supermarket has a very loose weave, making it suitable for only fresh cheeses. The advantage is that it is readily available and very inexpensive. Butter muslin is the alternative. It has a much tighter weave, is stronger, and is reusable as long as you rinse it in your sanitizer solution after use. The only drawback to butter muslin is that it is available only at cheese supply stores or online, so if you decide to make cheese on the spur of the moment you may be out of luck. For the basic cheeses included in this section, I have found that if I double over my inexpensive cheese cloth, things work out fairly well. However, when you move into the more advanced stages of cheese making, it is better to bite the bullet and get the butter muslin. Don't frustrate yourself by losing some potentially good cheese over cheap cheese cloth.

Thermometer: You will need a dairy thermometer; a candy thermometer will not work, because its temperature range is too high. An instant-read thermometer is sufficient, or you can use one that will attach to the side of the pot for a constant reading. If you want to go high-tech, an electronic, digital thermometer is a real winner because it has an alarm for precise settings. When using a double boiler, it is a good idea to have two thermometers going at the same time; this will give you better control over your milk temperature.

Although cheese as a food is generally safe to consume, it does have the potential to produce serious food illness, so it is best to follow basic sanitation procedures when making your own.

Techniques for Making Fresh, Soft Cheeses

The following steps for making fresh, soft cheeses are fairly simple. These cheeses are not molded or aged, and in the case of yogurt cheese, there is no need to heat the ingredients.

◀ Curding Milk: Acid Curd and Cultured Milk

In making any fresh cheese, the first major step is to curdle the milk, which separates the solids and liquids, so the liquid (whey) can be drained off. There are two methods of accomplishing this: the first is to use an acid, typically in the form of vinegar or citric acid; the second involves acidifying the milk with bacterial cultures. As a general rule, acid-curd cheeses are the fastest to make: they can be made in as little time as it takes to boil milk, which makes them an ideal first cheese to attempt. The acid-curd fresh cheeses included here are paneer and lemon cheese.

When making an acid curd cheese, begin by placing a cooking thermometer into the top of your double boiler, add water to the base, and set the top in place. Turn the burner to a medium setting. In the top of the double boiler, heat your milk slowly, for twenty to thirty minutes, until it reaches 170°F (77°C). Just as it reaches the target temperature, remove the top of the double boiler and set it into a basin of ice water to cool, adding ice to the basin as necessary to bring the milk to 70°F to 72°F (21°C–22°C). Remove the pan from the basin and wrap a towel around it to maintain the temperature. Add the starter culture your recipe calls for, and slowly stir to mix. Set the lid on the pan and allow the mixture to sit at room temperature for the length of time your recipe directs.

When making a fresh cheese with starter cultures, you will also need a double boiler, but the milk will be heated to a lower temperature, generally below 100°F (38°C) (check each recipe for the specific temperature). When you have reached the target temperature, add the amount of culture called for, stir, and wait for the curds to form.

TOOLS

Cooking pan, or double boiler

Cheese thermometer (an instant-read thermometer, or any thermometer that is calibrated to read in 2°F (1°C) increments)

Stainless-steel stirring spoon

Colander

Cheese cloth or a loose-mesh kitchen towel

Catch bowl

Cultured fresh cheeses come in many different varieties; the ones included here are chèvre, quark, yogurt, yogurt cheese, cream cheese, crème fraîche, and cottage cheese.

◄ Draining Curds

Line a colander with cheese cloth and place a catch bowl underneath. Use a piece of cheese cloth that is large enough to cover the cheese when it has finished draining.

Spoon the cheese curds from the double boiler into the cheese cloth-lined colander, fold the excess cheese cloth over the curds, and allow the whey to drain into the catch bowl for two hours.

Draining ►

Discard the whey from the colander, gather the cheese cloth into a ball, and tie off the ends around a wooden spoon. Let the cheese continue to drain, either refrigerated or at room temperature, according to your recipe instructions. Do not touch the whey for eight to twenty-four hours, as your recipe requires.

Finishing ►

After the cheese has drained enough to the desired consistency, remove it from the cheese cloth, roll it into a ball, and place it in a covered plastic container (or spoon into a covered container, depending on the consistency). Refrigerate your cheese for up to two weeks, or for as long as the recipe recommends.

Basic Cheese Recipes

In the recipes that follow, use cow's milk unless goat's milk is specified in the recipe. If you prefer the tangy flavor of goat's milk, it may be substituted for cow's milk in all of the recipes.

For a festive party or breakfast spread, make yogurt cheese from fruit-flavored yogurts, such as lemon, banana, and strawberry, and serve your cheese garnished with whole-fruit jams, such as sour cherry or blueberry.

Paneer

Paneer is a staple in Indian cooking. Go to any Indian restaurant and you are likely to find Saag Paneer, a scrumptious dish of spinach, curry, ghee, and of course, paneer. Often listed as a cottage cheese, it has a firmer structure that is actually more similar to tofu. Although it is possible to find paneer in specialty markets, the commercial variety tends to have a rubbery texture.

INGREDIENTS

10 cups (2.4 L) whole milk

6 tablespoons (90 ml) lemon juice or $1/2$ cup (125 grams) yogurt

TECHNIQUES

For tools and illustrated steps, see Techniques for Making Fresh, Soft Cheeses, page 48.

PROCEDURE

Bring milk to a boil over medium heat, being sure to stir frequently so it does not burn or form a skin on the bottom of the pan. When the milk begins to boil, turn down the heat and add the lemon juice or yogurt and stir. The milk should start separating into fluffy white curds and thin, watery whey. If the curds are not forming, add more juice or yogurt until the whey is almost clear.

When the curds start forming, immediately turn off the heat. This is important because the longer the curds stay on the heat the tougher they become. Strain the cheese mixture into a cheese cloth–lined colander, making sure you have a bowl under the colander to catch the whey. Tie the ends of the cheese cloth into a loose ball, and very gently squeeze to remove the additional whey.

Place the cheese ball onto a flat surface, such as a table or a counter-top, and place a heavy weight on top. The best approach is to use a plastic container filled with water. Let it sit out in the open for four hours or until it has a firm consistency.

Yield: 1 pound (450 g)

Fresh paneer is easy to make and has a creamy texture that is vastly superior to the denser texture of commercially made paneer.

Saag Paneer

Here is a simple version of Saag Paneer that will allow you to use your homemade cheese. Saag paneer is one of the most popular Indian dishes. Its savory spices blend perfectly with the soft textured cheese, making it a dish that is a treat·any time.

INGREDIENTS

14 ounces (400 g) paneer cut into ½" (about 1 cm) cubes

3 tablespoons (45 ml) vegetable oil

1½ pounds (680 g) frozen spinach, thawed and drained

8 tablespoons (120 g) ghee (see page 159 for recipe)

1 teaspoon (2 g) cumin seed

3 cloves peeled garlic, finely chopped

2 teaspoons (3 g) ground coriander

1 teaspoon (3 g) red chili powder

4 ounces (120 ml) cream

Salt

Heat vegetable oil in a sauté pan over medium heat, and fry paneer cubes until all sides are golden brown. Remove from the pan and set aside. Add two tablespoons of ghee to the pan, and sauté spinach for four to six minutes. Transfer to a blender and purée. Heat the remaining ghee over medium high heat, and add cumin seeds. Once they begin to crackle, stir in the chopped garlic and sauté until golden. Add coriander, chili powder, and spinach. Cook for 3 or 4 minutes, stirring constantly. Add paneer and simmer to heat. Stir in cream, and salt to taste. Serve immediately.

Serves 6

Fresh Chèvre

This fresh goat's cheese is easy to make and has a great flavor. Working with goat's milk is a little different from cow's milk, because the curds are softer and require some care when handling. If you are using pasteurized milk, or simply find that your curds are too soft and not holding up well, add calcium chloride.

INGREDIENTS

1/2 gallon (1.9 L) goat's milk

1/8 teaspoon (about 1 ml) direct-set culture

One drop of rennet dissolved in 5 tablespoons (28 ml) of unchlorinated water

Calcium chloride as needed (1/8 teaspoon [about 1 ml] diluted in 4 tablespoons [20 ml] of cool water (see page 72 for guidelines on using calcium chloride)

TECHNIQUES

For tools and illustrated steps, see Techniques for Making Fresh, Soft Cheeses, page 48.

PROCEDURE

Warm the milk to 72°F (22°C), then add the starter culture and mix well. Add one tablespoon (5 ml) of diluted rennet, and stir for two minutes. Cover and keep milk at the target temperature. Cheese curds will form in eighteen hours. If it looks like curds haven't formed after that time, let it set longer. Sometimes this step will take up to twenty-four hours.

Cut the curds and check for a clean break (for how to cut curds and check for a clean break, see page 83). When the curds cut cleanly, ladle them into a chees cloth–lined colander with the catch bowl underneath. Tie the cheese cloth into a ball, wrapping the ends around a wooden spoon to allow the whey to drain freely.

When the whey has stopped draining, the cheese is ready, usually within four to six hours. Take the cheese out of the cloth, package it in an airtight refrigerator container. Refrigerate for up to two weeks.

Yield: 1/2 pound (225 g)

Artisan Advice When making Chèvre, you will notice a layer of cream on top of the ripened milk, and that the whey has risen to the top. One of the unique characteristics of goat's milk is that it is naturally partially homogenized. This is another reason to add calcium chloride to the milk before ripening it in order to increase its yield. Although it will take some time for the curds to set, the milk is ready when you see a thin layer of cream form on the surface.

Chèvre Chaud

The French have a fantastic recipe for goat cheese called Chèvre Chaud (literally translated as hot goat cheese), which calls for breading fresh chèvre and frying it. Typically this dish is served with a salad and light vinaigrette. It is so common in France I often wonder why we don't see more of it here—it is delicious.

INGREDIENTS
11 ounces (310 g) fresh goat Chèvre
³/₄ cup (40 g) fresh bread crumbs
1 egg, beaten

Mold the goat cheese into two or four ¹/₂" (about 1 cm) -thick patties. Dip each patty into the beaten egg, and then coat it in fresh bread crumbs.

Place the cheese patties on a nonstick sheet pan and broil until lightly browned. Turn and brown the other side. When the cheese patties are lightly browned on both sides and soft in the center, remove and place them over a bed of mixed greens topped with a light vinaigrette dressing.

Yield: Two entrées, or four appetizers

Quark

Although Quark is virtually unknown in the United States, it is found in nearly every German household. Tangy like sour cream, with some additional body, it can be made with whole milk or low-fat milk, depending on your preference.

INGREDIENTS

1 gallon (3.8 L) milk

1/4 teaspoon (about 1 g) direct-set buttermilk culture, or 2 tablespoons (28 ml) buttermilk

TECHNIQUES

For illustrated steps, see Techniques for Making Fresh, Soft Cheeses, page 48.

PROCEDURE

Heat the milk to 88°F (31°C), and add the culture or starter, according to package directions.

After the milk and let it ripen at room temperature for twenty-four hours, or until the milk has set (it should have the consistency of a firm yogurt).

After the mixture sets, pour it into a cheese cloth–lined colander, tie it into a ball, and let it hang from a wooden spoon. Let the cheese drain in your refrigerator overnight, with a catch bowl placed underneath the colander. When the mixture has drained, remove it from the colander and the cheese cloth, place it in an air-tight refrigerator container, and store in the refrigerator for up to two weeks.

Yield: 1 pound (450 g)

Yogurt

Yogurt has been a staple for thousands of years in Eastern Europe, North Africa, India, and Central Asia; the word yogurt is Turkish in origin. This fermented milk product remained in relative obscurity in Western Europe until the early twentieth century, when it was discovered that the cultures used to make it provide significant health benefits. Now yogurt is a ubiquitous product found in a multitude of forms.

Making yogurt is a simple process, which allows you to produce fresh, tasty yogurt that costs half as much as what you pay in the store. Although yogurt itself is not a cheese, it can be made into cheese (see the recipe on page 60), and can also be used as a starter for making other cheeses.

INGREDIENTS

1 quart (0.9 L) milk (whole or low-fat)

1 packet (5 g) of yogurt starter (see Resources, page 173)

TECHNIQUES

For tools and illustrated steps, see Techniques for Making Fresh, Soft Cheeses, on page 48.

PROCEDURE

Heat the milk in a cooking pan to 180° F (82°C). As soon as it reaches this temperature, it should be removed from the burner. Cool the milk to 108°F–112°F (42°C–44°C).

In a measuring cup, dissolve the packet of starter culture in a small amount of milk. Pour this mixture into the pan of milk and stir. Cover and keep the milk at 116°F (47°C) for four to four and a half hours until the mixture has reached the desired consistency. Spoon the finished yogurt into an airtight container and refrigerate for up to two weeks.

Yield: 1 quart (0.9 l)

Variation: **Crème Bulgare**

Use the same procedure as for yogurt, but simply substitute light cream for milk.

Homemade yogurt is an easy-to-make, healthy, and delicious treat—and it can be used as a starter culture for making other fresh cheeses. When making cheese, save the watery whey for making ricotta cheese or for baking.

Yogurt Cheese

Yogurt cheese is one of the easiest cheeses to make. Its beauty lies in its simplicity; no special tools are required, and it can be made in as little as eight hours. Light and delicious, with a cream-cheese texture and a tangy flavor like that of sour cream, it has many uses. Although traditionally made with plain yogurt, try it with some of the flavored varieties, such as lemon, vanilla, or better yet, coffee.

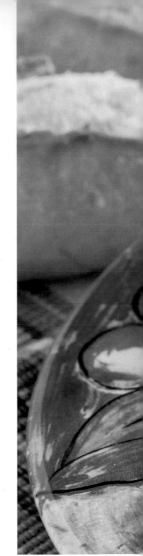

INGREDIENTS

2 pounds (0.9 grams) low-fat or nonfat yogurt

TECHNIQUES

For tools and illustrated steps, see Techniques for Making Fresh, Soft Cheeses, page 48.

PROCEDURE

Select a low-fat or nonfat yogurt variety labeled as containing live cultures. Do not use the Swiss- or custard-style yogurts, because they contain gelatin, which prevents the whey from separating from the yogurt and thus prevents it from forming cheese. You can use as much or as little yogurt as you like. Keep in mind that you'll get half as much cheese as the yogurt you put into it.

Line a colander with cheese cloth, and place a catch bowl underneath. Pour the yogurt into the lined colander, and spread the yogurt across the cheese cloth, taking care not to compress it. Cover the colander with a clean towel or plastic wrap, and set the yogurt, colander, and catch bowl in the refrigerator to drain.

Check on it after two hours; you should notice that a considerable amount of whey has drained from the yogurt into the catch bowl. Discard the whey (or save it for baking). Gather the cheese cloth into a ball, and tie the ends around a wooden spoon, as shown on page 84. Suspend the yogurt above a deep bowl or stock pot by resting the wooden spoon on the

rims of the container, so that there is room for whey to drain into the container.

Allow the bundle of cheese to continue draining in the refrigerator—without disturbing it—for another eight to twenty-four hours, until it reaches the desired consistency. After eight hours it will be a soft spread; at the twenty-four-hour mark, the yogurt cheese should have a consistency comparable to cream cheese.

Remove the cheese from the cloth, form it into a ball, and place it in a covered plastic container in the refrigerator. Stored this way, yogurt cheese should keep for up to two weeks.

Yield: 2 cups (400 g)

Cream Cheese

If you have never had fresh cream cheese, you are in for a treat. Virtually all of the commercially produced cream cheese contains stabilizers and gums that extend its shelf life. With this recipe you will have a wholly natural cream cheese, and you'll never need to shop for it at the supermarket.

INGREDIENTS

4 cups (950 ml) non-ultra pasteurized half and half

1 cup (235 ml) non-ultra pasteurized whipping cream

2 tablespoons (28 ml) buttermilk

Salt

Herbs (optional)

TECHNIQUES

For tools and illustrated steps, see Techniques for Making Fresh, Soft Cheeses, page 48.

PROCEDURE

Heat the creams to 90°F (32°C), then stir in the buttermilk and pour the mixture into a sanitized mixing bowl, preferably glass or any nonreactive metal. Cover the bowl with plastic wrap. Wrap a few kitchen towels around the bowl, making certain that they fit snugly. Place the bowl in a warm area, and let it sit for twenty-four hours.

After twenty-four hours, the cream mixture should have the consistency of yogurt and should not move when the bowl is leaned on its side. If it still has some movement, the cultures need more time to develop, so let it sit for another six to twelve hours. Once you have a firm mixture, pour it into your cheese cloth–lined colander with a catch bowl underneath. Allow it to drain for fifteen minutes, then fold the cheese cloth over the cheese. Place the colander in a deep bowl for continued draining. Cover it with plastic, and place in the refrigerator for as long as twelve to fourteen hours.

Remove the curd from the cheese cloth, and salt to taste. Add herbs if desired. Reshape the curds into balls and wrap them in fresh cheese cloth; put the balls back into the refrigerator in the colander. Make sure that you have a drip bowl under the colander to catch any additional whey. Cover the colander with plastic wrap, and let it sit for thirty-six to forty-eight hours, depending on the firmness of cheese you desire.

Place finished cheese in a sealed plastic container in the refrigerator. Stored this way, the cream cheese should last for up to two weeks.

Yield: 1 pound (450 g)

Homemade cream cheese has a fresh flavor and creamy texture that will make you wonder why anyone would go to the store for this breakfast treat.

Lemon Cheese

Delicious and simple, lemon cheese can be used as a light, refreshing spread. Add some fresh herbs, such as chives or dill, for additional zest.

INGREDIENTS

¹/₂ gallon (1.9 L) whole milk

¹/₄ cup (60 ml) fresh-squeezed lemon juice

TECHNIQUES

For tools and illustrated steps, see Techniques for Making Fresh, Soft Cheeses, page 48.

PROCEDURE

Heat the milk to 165°F (74°C), stirring frequently to prevent the milk from scorching. Once the milk reaches the target temperature, take the pot off the burner and stir in the lemon juice. Let the milk rest for fifteen minutes. The curds will partially separate in the milk. If you are using homogenized milk, the curds will appear as thin threads.

Pour the mixture into a cheese cloth–lined colander with a catch bowl underneath, and tie the cheese cloth into a ball. Place the colander, cheese, and catch bowl in the refrigerator, and allow the cheese to drain for one hour, or until the whey stops dripping. Remove the cheese from the refrigerator, unwrap the cloth, and put the cheese into a bowl. Salt to taste, and mix in any additional herbs you want. Place the cheese in an airtight container, and store it in the refrigerator for up to one week.

Yield: 1 pound (450 g)

Mascarpone

Here is an easy cheese to make that is so good you won't want to go to the store for it ever again. Although best known as an ingredient for the Italian desserts cannoli and tiramisu, this cheese has a plethora of other uses. Use it stuffed in raviolis, in cream sauces, or blended with coffee liquor to create a dip for biscotti.

INGREDIENTS

1 quart (0.9 L) light cream

1/4 teaspoon (about 1 g) direct-set crème fraîche culture

TECHNIQUES

For tools and illustrated steps, see Techniques for Making Fresh, Soft Cheeses, page 48.

PROCEDURE

Heat the milk to 86°F (30°C), then add the starter culture. Cover the milk, and let it ripen at room temperature for twelve hours, or until the milk has set (it will then have the consistency of a very thick yogurt).

Pour the mixture into a cheese cloth–lined colander set over a catch bowl. Drape the ends of the cheese cloth over the cheese, and place the cheese, colander, and bowl in the refrigerator. Let the cheese drain until it reaches the desired consistency, from creamy to spreadable. This process will take one to four hours. When the cheese has drained, remove from the cheese cloth, and store in an airtight container in the refrigerator for up to four weeks.

Yield: 1 pound (450 g)

Crème Fraîche

Crème fraîche is technically a cultured dairy product rather than a cheese. Nonetheless, it is an exceptional product with many uses. Crème fraîche is a staple in a French kitchen because it adds depth of flavor to sauces.

INGREDIENTS

1 quart (0.9 L) light cream

¼ teaspoon (about 1 g) direct-set crème fraîche starter culture (see Resources, page 173)

TECHNIQUES

For tools and illustrated steps, see Techniques for Making Fresh, Soft Cheeses, page 48.

PROCEDURE

Heat the cream to 86°F (30°C). Add the starter culture, stir, and let sit at room temperature for twelve hours, or until coagulated.

When set, spoon it into an airtight container and store in the refrigerator for up to one week.

Yield: 1 pound (450 g)

Artisan Advice

Crème fraîche is more versatile than many dairy products. It is a natural accompaniment to a range of foods including fresh fruit and smoked fish; it can be used as an alternative to sour cream for cream sauces. Because crème fraîche contains 10 percent more fat than sour cream, and consequently less protein, it will hold up to higher temperatures that other fermented dairy products cannot.

Crème fraîche is a versatile substitute for fresh or sour cream in savory sauces, casseroles, or dips. For topping desserts, it can be whipped like fresh cream.

Cottage Cheese

Cottage cheese is simple to make, economical, and versatile—you can add any flavoring you like, typically fruits or herbs.

Cottage cheese, pot cheese, Dutch cheese, and Schmierkase are all the same names for this soft, uncured cheese that is such a staple in North America. Cottage cheese is traditionally made with skim milk, but it can also be made with whole milk. In addition, cream can be added for more flavor, in which case the end product would carry the name creamed cottage cheese.

INGREDIENTS

1 gallon (3.8 L) skim or whole milk

Calcium chloride ($1/8$ teaspoon [about 1 ml] diluted in $1/4$ cup [60 ml] water [see page 72])

$1/8$ teaspoon (about 1 ml) mesophilic direct-set culture

Cheese salt (optional)

Heavy cream (optional)

TECHNIQUES

For tools and illustrated steps, see Techniques for Making Fresh, Soft Cheeses, page 48.

PROCEDURE

Heat the milk to 72°F (22°C), then add the calcium chloride. (If you are using homogenized milk, the suggested amount of calcium chloride is $1/8$ teaspoon [about 1 g] diluted in $1/4$ cup [30 ml] cool water per 1 gallon [3.8 L] of milk. Add the starter culture, stir well, and cover. Let the milk ripen for twenty-four hours at room temperature. Be certain that the milk does not fall below 68°F (20°C). After the curds set, cut them into $1/4$" (4 mm) cubes, and let rest for fifteen minutes.

Put the pot on the stove, and heat the curds to 100°F (38°C); this should take twenty-five minutes. Stir occasionally to keep the curds from matting. Keep the curds at 100°F (38°C) for an additional ten minutes and continue to stir. Slowly increase the temperature of the curds to 112°F (44° C) for fifteen minutes. Hold at this target temperature for an additional thirty minutes. Check the curds for consistency. They should be firm, not soft and mushy. If they are still soft,

they need be cooked longer—check again in five minutes. When they reach the right consistency, let them rest for five minutes.

Pour the curds into a cheese cloth–lined colander, and tie the cloth into a ball. Dunk the ball into a bowl of cold water several times to eliminate any additional whey, which can make the cheese sour. Set the ball into a colander with a catch bowl underneath, and let the whey drain for five minutes. In a bowl of ice water, rinse the cheese-cloth bundle of curds again, and let them drain in the colander for another five minutes.

Untie the cheese cloth and break apart any large curd pieces. If you want a creamier cheese, blend in one to two tablespoons of heavy cream. Salt to taste. Place the cheese in an airtight container, and store in your refrigerator for up to two weeks.

Yield: 1 pound (450 g)

CHAPTER FOUR
Intermediate Cheese Making

The cheeses in this chapter cover a broad range of varieties. If cheeses such as Cheddar and Swiss Emmental are to your liking, then look no further. The cheeses covered in this chapter fall into three categories: pressed cheeses, such as Cheddar and Romano; washed-curd cheeses such as Gouda and Colby; and pasta filata cheeses such as Mozzarella and Provolone.

Before you begin to make these cheeses, it should be pointed out that unlike fresh cheeses, which require very little equipment, and can be made rather quickly and consumed almost immediately, the cheeses found in this section are more time consuming, require additional equipment and ingredients, and generally take months to ripen. They are truly to be made with delayed gratification in mind. Yet making these cheeses is a very satisfying experience. Think about it—when you are making Gouda, you are using techniques that are centuries old. Though the equipment and ingredients are updated for modern times, the principles remain the same. In a strange metaphysical way, it is as if you are in touch with cheese makers throughout history when you are making these cheeses.

Cheeses that meet with universal approval include many molded cheeses, such as Cheddar, Colby, and Monterey Jack with peppers, which are discussed in this chapter. Waxing these finished cheeses extends their shelf life, locks in moisture, and prevents them from molding.

Annatto coloring, which is derived from seeds of a Central American plant, is used to give Cheddar and Colby cheeses their characteristic yellow or orange coloring.

Ingredients

Making these cheeses will require you to purchase some ingredients in addition to the ones listed in the previous chapter. Other than milk, the necessary ingredients, such as penicillium molds for ripening, rennet, and cheese starter cultures, are generally not readily available in your local grocery store and will need to be purchased through a cheese-making supply company, several of which are listed in the Resources section on page 172.

Annatto Coloring

Have you ever wondered how some cheeses, particularly Colby and Cheddar, get that brilliant orange color? Well, the milk certainly did not come out of the cow that way; something was added—namely annatto coloring. Annatto is a food colorant that comes from the seed of the bush *Bixa orellana,* which is native to Central America. The waxy coatings on the seeds carry pigments of red, yellow, and orange. Cows that graze on grains and silage, rather than fresh grasses, produce pale-colored milk, and annatto was originally added to compensate for this. (In some cases there seems to be overcompensation, because some colored cheeses look almost phosphorescent.) Although purists might turn up their noses as using annatto, some cheeses are closely associated with this coloring and may look "off" without it.

Calcium Chloride

Milk that is mass-produced and available in the local supermarket has taken a beating before getting on the shelf. The processes of homogenizing and high-temperature pasteurizing have a negative effect on the calcium balance, which will negatively affect rennet activity when making cheese. In order to correct this imbalance, you need to add calcium to the milk in the form of calcium chloride. If you plan on using regular milk, it is almost imperative to add calcium chloride; otherwise, you will find that your curd structure is too soft to make cheese. (The suggested amount is 1/8 teaspoon [about 1 ml] per gallon of milk diluted in 1/4 cup [about 60 ml] of cool water.)

Starter Cultures: Mother Culture and Direct-Set Cultures

When making intermediate to advanced cheeses, you must use starter cultures to initiate the acidification of the milk. As previously mentioned, starter cultures are various strains of bacteria that are added to milk to change the acidity level, thereby allowing the solids to separate from the milk with the assistance of rennet. Two types of starter cultures are available to the cheese maker: mother cultures and direct-set cultures.

Mother Cultures

Using mother cultures is the traditional way of making cheese. Historically, these cultures were perpetuated by saving a small amount of milk or whey from the previous day's work and storing it for future use. Once cultivated, a mother culture can be used repeatedly, hence the name "mother." Traditionally, a mother culture represented local bacteria from where the cheese was was made, giving the cheese a flavor profile unique to that particular region of the world. Think of this in the same way that a type of wine, or its qualities, can change within a particular region of the world, even though vintners in various regions use the same grapes.

American, or Processed Cheeses

Let's face it: For many of us, our first experience with cheese was eating processed slices from individually wrapped packages. And although there will not be a recipe for this kind of cheese found in this book, for the sake of education, let's take a quick look at how processed cheeses are made.

Processed cheeses are the new kids on the block in the cheese world. They were first developed in 1911, and are popular with the large cheese producers because they are inexpensive to make, have a long shelf life, and create minimum waste. They are produced by shredding a blend of cheeses and then combining them with water, additional flavorings, and emulsifying salts. The mix is then heated in the range of 158°F to 194°F (70°C–90°C) and poured into portion molds. The emulsifying salts act as a binder to keep the cheeses from losing moisture and oil during the heating process. Although this process provides an interesting look at the world of science, one cannot vouch for the flavor of the end result of this experiment.

Single-serve slices of processed cheese are among the earliest memories of many cheese lovers.

Mother culture is a thick, yogurtlike mixture of milk and starter culture for making cheeses. Once made, it can keep for up to three months in the freezer.

Mother cultures are more difficult to use than direct-set cultures because they take time and effort to cultivate. For the beginning cheese maker, it is best to start off using the direct-set cultures until you become accustomed to the cheese-making process. But for the sheer romance of cheese making, there is nothing like the authentic feel of a home-grown starter culture.

PREPARING MOTHER CULTURE

EQUIPMENT
One quart (0.9 L) canning jar
One quart (0.9 L) skim milk
Mother culture starter
Canning kettle, or large cooking pot

SANITIZING JARS
Fill the cooking pot about three-quarters full of water, and bring it to a boil over high heat. Place your jars in the boiling water for five minutes. Be certain that each jar and lid is fully immersed in the water and that there are no air pockets.

PREPARING MILK FOR MOTHER CULTURE
To prepare a mother culture, you will need quart-sized jars. Canning jars work well due to their wide mouth and ease of cleaning. Sterilize them in your cooking pot; first, ensure that they will fit into the pot, so that they will be completely covered with boiling water.

Sterilizing Milk   *You will need to sterilize the milk used in creating a mother culture to prevent any foreign bacteria from ruining your culture. Place the sealed jars filled with milk into a pot deep enough to cover the entire jars and lids. Put on a slow boil and wait for twenty minutes.*

Inoculating Medium   *Once the milk has cooled to the proper temperature of 75°F (25°C) for mesophilic cultures and 110°F (43°C) for thermophilic cultures, add your starter culture, seal the jar with the lid, and gently agitate. Keep the sealed jars at the proper temperature (75°F [25°C] for mesophilic and 110°F [43°C] for themophilic) for a minimum of fifteen hours for a mesophilic culture and four hours for a thermophilic culture. After that, you should have a jar full of something that looks like yogurt.*

Finished Cultures   *Keep your culture refrigerated for a week and then store it in the freezer for up to three months. After a week, any mother culture that you do not use needs to be stored in the freezer. The suggested method is to use sanitized ice cube trays. The standard size will produce 1 ounce (28 g) portions, which are the perfect size for use. You can use the cubed cultures for up to three months, after which time you will need to propagate again.*

Fill the cooking pot about three-quarters full of water, and bring to a boil over high heat. Place empty jars in the boiling water, for five minutes. Be certain that the entire jars and lids are immersed in the water and that there are no air pockets in them.

Direct-Set Cultures

This type of culture is a modern creation, in which the essential bacteria are isolated and cultivated in a laboratory. They have many of the characteristics found in a mother culture, without the effort of having to cultivate and store it. Direct-set cultures are intended for single use only, so they cannot be used for creating a mother culture. However, they are tremendously convenient for the average home cheese maker. All you do is simply buy the culture, store in your freezer, and then add it to the prepared milk as called for in each recipe. Direct-set cultures are available through a variety of cheese-making suppliers listed in the Resources section of this book on page 172.

Rennet

As discussed previously, rennet is used in conjunction with the starter culture; rennet allows the curd particles to form into a solid mass (see page 83). A number of rennet varieties are available, and they typically break down into two groups: animal rennet and vegetable rennet. Generally speaking, the animal-derived rennet tends to work best, providing a solid, tight curd. Vegetable rennet is also very effective for making cheese; however, it will give a slightly bitter flavor to an aged cheese.

Whichever rennet you choose, you must be certain that you dilute it in 1/4 cup (60 ml) of cool, unchlorinated water before adding it to the milk. This practice encourages the proper distribution of rennet throughout the milk.

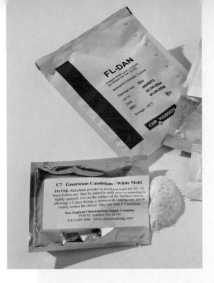

Commercial starter cultures are convenient to use and take the worry out of accurate measurements of starter cultures for the home cheese maker.

➤ Rennet: Liquid or Tablet Form?

Rennet comes in two forms: a liquid and a tablet. Both are effective, and each one has certain benefits and drawbacks. Tablets have an indefinite shelf life, which make them ideal for the person who is not making cheese on a frequent basis. The drawback with the tablets is that they are not the most precise way of measuring, and they are not easily rehydrated in water. Conversely, liquid rennet is very precise to measure, which makes it simple to use, but it has a shelf life of only a year when kept in the refrigerator.

Equipment

Getting started in more advanced cheese making requires additional tools. Most of these tools are available at one of the cheese-making supply companies listed in the Resources section on page 172.

Depending on your skill level and inclination, you may want to make do with what you have around the house. This is not too absurd if you think about it, because for hundreds of years, cheese was made with tools that would be rejected by today's modern sanitation requirements. Again, simple common sense is all you need. Be certain that you keep your equipment clean before and after you make your cheese. When using plastic materials, stick with food-grade plastic, also known as polypropylene. If you have any doubt about whether a tool is food safe, then don't use it. It is better to err on the side of caution than to ruin your cheeses.

Cheese Press

The cheese press is the essential tool needed to make hard cheeses. A wide variety of presses is available through cheese-making supply houses. One that is most interesting is the Wheeler-style press from New England Cheese Making Supply. It has a stately, rustic look about it that says, "I'm a cheese press." The others worth looking at are the CHEESEYPRESS and the SEESEYPRESS from Jack Schmidling Products.

If you want to make your own press, there are countless sources of patterns and instructions. New England Cheese Making Supply offers such information. There is also an interesting example on the Web from David Fankhauser. He has made a press using chopsticks, industrial-strength rubber bands, and a cooking pot. Truly an inventive guy!

A cheese press is a simple device that applies pressure to cheese that is inside a perforated mold. As the pressure is increased, watery whey drains out and is discarded, and the wheel of cheese solidifies and takes on its permanent shape.

Curd Knife

This tool is simply a long knife that can reach to the bottom of the pot to cut your curds. Ideally you are looking for a thin blade that will cut in clean lines. Specially made curd knives are available from cheesemaking suppliers (see Resources, page 172), or you can experiment with a similarly shaped kitchen knife, such as a ham slicer.

Cheese Board

Cheese boards are cutting boards that you will need for drying your cheese after it comes out of the cheese press. Sterilize the board with a steam bath for twenty minutes before each use. Do not use a plastic board, because it will not absorb any of the moisture from the cheese.

pH Testing Equipment

As mentioned earlier, knowing the proper acidity of milk is essential for the success of your cheese. There are several ways to measure this. The easiest and least expensive way is to purchase those famous pH strips that everyone used in high school science class. They are cheap and effective. If you are inclined to more precise measurements, you

A simple cutting board of unfinished wood is the best material to use for drying cheese, because it absorbs excess moisture from the base of the cheese.

should look at the various gadgets that are available. One of the more interesting tools to come out is an instant-read pH tester. Battery-operated with an LCD display, it can give you a reading in a matter of seconds. No fuss, no muss—it is ideal for the striving "cheese head," and it makes a great gift.

Ripening Cave

It is essential that you create the right environment in which your cheese can mature. It would be a shame to take all of the time and effort that went into making a cheese and then blow it because the cheese was not properly ripened. Remember that cheese is a living, breathing organism and must be handled accordingly. Let's look at what it takes to ripen a cheese at home.

THE MODERN CHEESE CAVE, A.K.A HOME REFRIGERATOR

Throughout history, cheeses were ripened in cool, dark places, such as caves or cellars. If you ever walk into a cave, one thing you will notice is just how darn damp it is. Cold and clammy, caves are ideal for ripening cheese, because cheeses prefer an average temperature of 45°F to 60°F (7°C–16°C), with a relative humidity of anywhere from 75 to 95 percent. Looking at these criteria, you can immediately see that there is going to be a problem with using your kitchen refrigerator as a ripening cave. The fridge at home, which is likely set at about 40°F (5°C), is too cold to allow the starter culture to develop properly.

The ideal environment for ripening cheeses is a cave, and for centuries it was the only way to ripen cheeses. But for the home cheese maker, a dedicated refrigerator, such as an inexpensive under-the-counter model—or for bigger batches, a full-sized "garage" fridge—will do an admirable job of cheese ripening.

The best alternative is to look into purchasing a small refrigerator for your cheese ripening. In choosing your home "cave," it is better to start large rather than small. If a full-sized Subzero is out of the question, however, a medium-sized refrigerator will do; it all depends on what amount of cheese you are planning to make. Even one of those small college-dorm refrigerators will work, but keep in mind that they are small, so you will be limited in what you can make and how long you can store it.

REFRIGERATOR THERMOSTAT Once you have decided on your cave, your next purchase should be a refrigerator thermostat (see Resources, on page 172). This nifty little contraption allows you to override the thermostat inside the refrigerator and has a temperature range of 30°F to 80°F (–1°C–27°C). Because no refrigerator manufacturer would ever dream of setting a unit at 60° F (16°C), an external thermostat is a must.

HUMIDISTAT Getting moisture into your cave is easy; a small pan of water will do. However, knowing that your cheeses are being properly hydrated is a different story. If you put the effort into making cheese and building a cave, you better make sure that your cheeses flourish during ripening. In order to do this, you need a humidistat—an inexpensive and readily available tool found at hardware stores or on the Web.

A refrigerator thermostat will allow you to set the temperature at the exact level needed to ripen the cheeses of your choice.

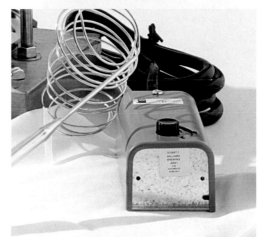

A humidistat will give you an accurate reading of the humidity in your ripening cave. The one pictured here includes a thermometer.

Cheese molds come in many shapes and sizes, and many of them have special shapes that are historically linked to certain types of cheeses.

Cheese Molds

The shape of a cheese is a direct result of the mold. Molds are perforated plastic forms that are used to hold the curd for draining. Cheese-making suppliers have a wide variety of shape and size choices, which are most often based on the traditional shapes called for in the recipes. A cheaper alternative is to use any of the ubiquitous food-grade plastic tubs. Take a medium-sized deli cup with a series of holes punched through (by you), and voilà, you have a cheese mold.

Cheese Follower

The cheese follower is a thin, flat piece of plastic that rests on top of your cheese. The follower is slightly smaller in diameter than the mold, so that it travels downward in the mold when pressure is applied. By evenly distributing the weight of the press over the surface of the cheese, a follower allows for a symmetrical cheese.

Cloth Banding, Natural Rind, or Waxing

When making aged cheeses, you will need a way to protect the outside of the cheese. There are three typical approaches: natural cloth banding, natural ring, and waxing. Cloth banding is the traditional way that cheeses are preserved. Quite simply, a cloth bandage is wrapped around the cheese, allowing for the formation of a rind.

A natural rind is formed when a cheese is allowed to sit in a ripening room for an extended period of time. The natural evaporation of the moisture from the cheese hardens the exterior, forming an impenetrable crust. When forming natural rinds, it is best to keep the cheeses clean with frequent washings or brushings with a mild brine solution (see page 86 for directions for making a brine solution).

Waxing is used to keep a cheese from drying out and to prevent mold growth on the exterior of your cheese. Although wax is breathable, it does not allow a full exchange of moisture the way a cloth

A coating of wax helps cheese retain moisture while excluding mold, and prolongs the storage life of the various cheeses.

band will. On the other hand, if you prefer a cheese that is softer with more moisture, waxing may be the way to go. The procedures for waxing are simple.

WAXING CHEESE

EQUIPMENT

2 pots (one for your cheese wax,
and the second to act as the double boiler)
Cheese thermometer
Cheese wax

PROCEDURE

1. Make sure that the cheese is sufficiently dry and cool.
2. Place the cheese wax in the wax pot, and melt it over a double boiler. Heat the wax to 250°F (121°C) to eliminate any surface bacteria that may have formed on the cheese.
3. Once the target temperature is reached, hold your cheese by the side and dip one half of it into the wax using a simple in-and-out motion. Let the wax dry and harden, and then dip and coat the other side. (See illustration at right.) Let the wax cool. Check for any spots you may have missed and repeat again, taking care to cover the entire cheese. Two coats are sufficient.

Cheese Trier

This funky little tool is essential for making any of the hard cheeses. As the name implies, the trier is used to sample a section of the cheese without having to cut it open. You simply core out a sample to taste and inspect. Break off a piece close to the center of the cheese, and then plug the cheese with the remainder. The cheese will fill in the small amount that was lost.

Mini Fan

This optional aid will discourage the formation of mold in the refrigerator, and will evenly distribute humidity. Set it in an area away from the cheese, close the door on the cord, and plug it into an outlet.

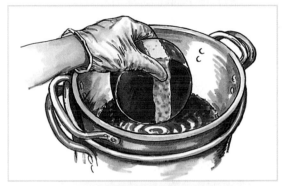

Although cheese wax is convenient for covering your cheese, it is difficult to clean out of your cooking pot. Why not save yourself the trouble and go to your local thrift shop and purchase a few inexpensive, stainless-steel cooking pots and reserve them for waxing?

Cheese makers guard their cheese trier as if it were made of precious metal, and for good reason. This simple stainless-steel tool is used to extract a small sample of cheese from the center of the wheel, so that the maker can taste it to judge its ripeness.

Intermediate Cheese-Making Techniques

◄ Culturing the Milk

This is the first stage in the cheese-making process. Also known as acidifying, the procedure entails adding the starter to the milk at the proper temperature and letting the culture grow. It is important that the milk is at the proper temperature and that this temperature is maintained throughout the process. The best way to assure this is to heat the milk in a hot-water bath (the kitchen sink works best). In general, the water needs to be ten degrees higher than your target temperature.

Additives to the Milk

After culturing your milk, it is time to add any of the additives required. Typically these include calcium chloride, annatto coloring, or lipase. When adding these to your milk, they need to be diluted in 1/4 cup (60 ml) cool water so that they are distributed evenly throughout the milk. Make sure that you stir the milk for a minute after adding them.

Renneting

No matter what type of rennet you use (dry or liquid), it needs to be diluted for even distribution throughout the milk. Use 1/4 cup (60 ml) cool, unchlorinated water. (Read the labels of bottled water to be sure it is unchlorinated.) If you are using rennet tablets, let them sit in the water for forty minutes before use.

The milk must be at the temperature stated in your recipe before adding the rennet. Rennet is effective between 68°F and 122°F (20°C–50°C). When adding the rennet to the milk, gently stir in circles and from top to bottom, for about one minute. If you are using raw milk or non-homogenized milk, you will need to top-stir as well. This method entails using your spoon and stirring the top half of the pot. In these types of milk, the cream rises to the top, and top-stirring assures an even distribution of rennet. Cover and wait the recommended time—in most cases thirty to forty minutes.

TOOLS

Cooking pan, or double boiler

Cheese thermometer

Stainless-steel stirring spoon

Colander

Cheese cloth

Catch bowl

Cheese press

Curd knife

Cheese board

pH testing strips, or electronic reader

Ripening cave (dedicated refrigerator)

Refrigerator thermostat

Humidistat

Cheese mold

Cheese follower

Cheese wax or butter muslin for banding

Two drying mats
(plastic or bamboo sushi mats)

Ripening box (a plastic food-grade box with sealing lid, or a large zip-close plastic bag)

Catch pan

Cheese film

8" x 8" (20 x 20 cm) baking pan

Molds

Checking for a Clean Break

After you have allowed the rennet to work on the ripened milk, you must check if your curds have reached the right consistency before you cut them. Too soon, and they will be mushy, and will lack the body necessary to successfully make cheese. Too late, and they won't cut cleanly. The best way to gauge curd development is to look for a clean break. This is done by placing your finger (make sure it's clean!) into the curds at about a 45 degree angle and pulling upward. If the curds lift, and break around your finger, then the curds are ready to cut. If they do not break, wait a few minutes and try again. Instead of your finger, you can use a knife, but you won't get the feel of the curds.

▼ Cutting the Curd

Cutting the curd takes place once the rennet has come to a complete set. The process of cutting is simple: Using your curd knife, cut rows ½" (about 1 cm) apart. Next, turn your pot 90 degrees, and using the same spacing, cut at right angles to your original cuts. The final cut is tricky, because you are trying to break the curd into cubes. The best approach is to use your knife to cut through half of the pot at a 45-degree angle. Turn the pot 90 degrees again, and finish cutting so that you have cheese pieces shaped roughly like cubes. When you start cutting, you will notice a tremendous release of whey. This is syneresis: the contraction of the curd and the release of the whey.

Remember that the size of the curds will affect the texture of the cheese. Smaller curds will result in a drier, firmer cheese, whereas larger curds will create a cheese with a smoother, softer texture. In the case of Swiss Emmental, ¼" (6 mm) is the standard size to cut the curd, about the size of a piece of long-grain rice. Traditionally, the

curds of Camembert are ladled into the molds in large unbroken pieces, and there is no cutting. These two cheeses could not be more dissimilar: Camembert with its smooth velvety texture, and Emmental with its tight, firm texture.

Artisan Advice It is important to cut cheese curds as close as possible to the size that the recipe calls for. If you have different-sized curds, some will turn out drier and others moister, which can lead to problems with the acidity of your cheese as well as its texture. Take your time when cutting curds: You only get one chance to do it right.

⇝ Using Direct-Set Cultures

There are a variety of sources from which you can purchase direct-set cultures. In some cases the suppliers will provide you with a single, prepackaged amount of culture that is ready for use, based on two gallons of milk. All you do is add the starter to the milk and stir. In other instances, suppliers sell bulk amounts that are intended for commercial use. In these instances, you will need to measure the culture using the suggested guidelines:

⅛ teaspoon per 1 gallon (3.8 L) milk
¼ teaspoon per 2–5 gallons (7.6–19 L) milk
½ teaspoon per 5–10 gallons (19–37.8 L) milk

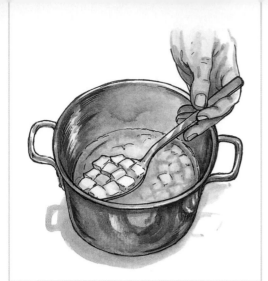

◄ Scalding and Stirring Curds

After renneting, the next step is to remove as much whey from the cheese as required. The whey contains lactic acid, which is the food for the starter culture. If the whey is not removed, the curds will become too acidic to make cheese with. The process for removing the whey involves scalding and stirring.

Scalding raises the temperature of the cut curds to a target temperature specific to the type of cheese being made. As the temperature rises, the rate of the whey draining from the curds increases. This has an added benefit of depriving the starter culture of nutrients, effectively slowing down its rate of growth. The longer the curds stay at the target temperature, the smaller the curds will become and the drier the cheese will be.

In conjunction with the scalding is the stirring of the curds. Stirring is done so that the curd particles are kept in suspension in the kettle or pot. Without stirring, the curds would combine and form large clumps, which will hinder the release of the whey and give the cheese an inconsistent texture.

◄ Removing the Whey by Draining

Draining is the final step in removing the whey from the curds. Typically it is done in a colander lined with cheese cloth or butter muslin. The procedure is simple: Once your curds have reached the desired texture, you simply pour your cut curds into the cheese cloth–lined colander and let gravity do all of the work.

In some cases you may want to tie the cheese cloth into a ball around the cheese, and hang it from a wooden spoon that rests on the edges of a stock pot.

In other cases, your next step is to remove the curds from the pan and place them directly into a mold for pressing. When making Cheddar or washed-curd cheeses, an additional step is required.

Milling

Milling is the process of breaking apart the drained curd with your hands into small pieces of a uniform size before preparing it for salting. The size of the pieces will affect the texture and flavor of the cheese as well as the amount of salt that needs to be added.

Salting

As mentioned earlier, salt plays a variety of roles in cheese making: as a preservative, a flavor enhancer, and a dehydrator. For the cheeses covered in this chapter, there are two methods for salting.

DRY-SALTING Typically associated with British-style cheeses such as Cheddar and Cheshire, dry-salting entails mixing dry salt with the curds at the end of the draining process, before placing the cheese in the mold and press. Typically, this process is done by sprinkling salt into the curds and mixing it with your hands. Once blended into the curds, the salt will help to shrink the curd pieces through dehydration, allowing the curds to knit closer together in the mold.

◄ **BRINE-SALTING** A brine is a supersaturated solution of salt and water, in which cheeses are literally bathed. (Brine solution consists of 2 pounds [905 g] of salt stirred into and dissolved in 1 gallon [4.5 L] of water, heated to 190°F [88°C].) The types of cheeses that are usually brined are hard cheeses, such as Gouda and Emmental. Brining occurs directly after a cheese is removed from the press. The cheese is literally dunked into this salty bath. Once in the brine, the cheese begins to absorb salt, and the proteins begin to harden and form the rind.

Pressing ▶

Pressing is the final stage in whey removal and the process that gives cheese its shape and texture. Pressing is a necessary step for all of the firm to hard cheeses, such as Cheddar, Gouda, and Emmental. When pressing your cheeses, keep in mind it is a delicate balance between too much and not enough pressure. A cheese that is underpressed will become too dense because the whey will not have a chance to drain properly. Too much pressure will cause the outer rind to split, allowing bacteria to ferment under the rind.

In general, the warmer the curds, the lighter the pressure required, because the whey will move more freely out of warmer curds. Although there are specific suggestions for pressing in each recipe, the general guideline is that for a harder cheese, you will want a longer pressing time. High-fat cheeses will also require a longer pressing time, because the fat retains more moisture. On your initial pressing, the draining fluid should be clear in color with a slow, steady flow. If the fluid has a milky white color, you are using too much pressure.

Cheese Turning

Turning is not a difficult concept, but it is an important one. Cheese turning simply means flipping your cheese over, end to end. Without turning the cheese, gravity will pull the moisture, fat, and proteins down to the bottom of the round, making your cheese lopsided with an uneven texture and flavor. In the beginning stages of aging, you will be turning the cheese frequently, as directed by the recipe. For the mature, ripened cheeses, you will do it once a week. This process allows you to keep an eye on your beloved and to let oxygen get to the bottom of the cheese, preventing rot from developing on the rind.

In general, the warmer the curds, the lighter the pressure required, because the whey will move more freely out of warmer curds.

Intermediate Cheese Recipes

You can make cheese in almost any kitchen, so don't call in the contractors if you feel yours is too small. Take a few moments to prepare your surroundings, because it is not advisable to prepare any other food while you are in the middle of making cheese.

- Remove all other food products. You don't want that leftover meatball landing in your pot of freshly made curds.

- Get rid of all your used dish cloths and towels. Bring in clean, unused ones, and have more than you think you need. It's better to have too many than not enough.

- Clean and sanitize your work surfaces. Start with soap and water, and finish off with a sanitizing solution.

- Lay out all your tools to make sure that you have everything you need.

- Change your clothes if they happen to be exceptionally dirty. Although you don't have to be fanatical about it, you wouldn't want to make cheese in the same shirt that you wore to mow the lawn.

Savory, salty, firm cheeses with flavor, color, and texture, such as Parmesean, Cheddar, and Monterey Jack, are not difficult to make—all that's needed are a few specialized tools and ingredients.

Monterey Jack is a popular snack cheese. The addition of dried red peppers transforms this favorite into crowd-pleasing Pepper Jack.

Monterey Jack cheese was brought to America from Spain, via Mexico, by the Franciscan monks in the eighteenth century. Originally known as Queso del Pais, it was a locally produced cheese in the Monterey area of California. One of the producers, Domingo Pedrazzi, created a cheese using a cheese press called a "housejack," which is where the name Jack was derived.

INGREDIENTS

2 gallons (7.6 L) whole milk

4 tablespoons (60 ml) mesophilic mother culture, or ¼ teaspoon (about 2 ml) mesophilic direct-set culture

⅛ teaspoon (about 1 ml) calcium chloride, diluted in ¼ cup (60 ml) cool water (see page 72 for guidelines on using calcium chloride)

½ teaspoon (5 ml) liquid rennet, or ½ tablet dry rennet diluted in cool, unchlorinated water

1 tablespoon (6 g) cheese salt

TECHNIQUES

For illustrated steps and tools, see Intermediate Cheese-Making Techniques, page 82.

PROCEDURE

Heat the milk to 88°F (31°C), then add the starter culture, stir, and cover. Raise the temperature to 90°F (32°C) and hold for thirty minutes. After culturing, only if you are using homogenized milk, add the calcium chloride.

Maintaining the target temperature of 90° F (32°C), add the diluted rennet and stir for one minute. Cover and let sit for forty-five minutes. Make a test cut with a curd knife to check for a clean break (see page 83). Cut the curds into ¼" (6 mm) cubes. Maintaining the target temperature, stir the curds for forty minutes.

Gradually raise the temperature to 100°F (38°C). This should take about thirty-five minutes. Stir frequently to keep the curds from matting. Once the target temperature is reached, maintain for thirty minutes, and continue stirring. Let the curds rest for five minutes.

Pour off the whey to the level of the curds, taking care not to lose any of the curds. Let the curds rest for an additional thirty minutes, stirring frequently to prevent the curds from matting. While the curds rest, make sure the target temperature is maintained. Line a colander with sterilized

Variation: Pepper Jack

A spicy alternative that is sure to wake up your mouth, Pepper Jack is perfect for any south-of-the border dish. Follow the recipe for Monterey Jack, with the following modifications.

ADDITIONAL INGREDIENTS
1 teaspoon (about 1 g) hot chili flakes
½ cup (120 ml) water

PROCEDURE Boil pepper flakes in water for fifteen minutes. Strain and remove the chili flakes, and set aside the water. (You will add this water to your milk.) Add the pepper water to the milk, then heat milk mixture. Add the starter culture. Add boiled pepper flakes when you are blending in the salt.

cheese cloth, and rest the colander over a deep bowl. Spoon the curds into the colander, and toss in the salt. Let the curds drain for five minutes.

Line a 2-pound (900 g) mold with cheese cloth, and fill it with the curds. Cover the curds with cheese cloth, top with a follower, and press at ten pounds for fifteen minutes. Remove the cheese from the press, and slowly, carefully unwrap it. Turn the cheese over, rewrap it in the cloth, and press at thirty pounds for thirty minutes. Repeat the unwrapping and turning procedure, this time pressing at forty pounds for twelve hours.

Remove the cheese from the press, and take it out of the mold. Unwrap the cheese cloth, and place the cheese on a cheese board. Let it air-dry at room temperature, turning it twice daily, until it is dry to the touch (usually within two to five days). Wax or oil the cheese and allow it to ripen for one to three months in a humid refrigerator at 55°F (13°C) and 80–85 percent humidity. Turn weekly.

Yield: 2 pounds (900 g)

Using Indirect Heat

Many cheese recipes call for a slow rise in temperature during the heating process. For these recipes, an indirect heat source is preferable, such as a hot-water bath or double boiler. In large cheese factories, a steam bath is used, giving an almost instantaneous response to address temperature fluctuations. A water bath is effective for heating, but keep in mind that there is a lag time between heating the water and the milk. A good rule of thumb is to aim to raise the water to ten degrees above the target temperature, and then maintain it at an equal number to maintain the cheese at the target temperature. With a water bath, it is a good idea to have two thermometers working—one in the water and one in the cheese—to avoid any mishaps.

Cotswold

Cotswold is a variation of the English cheese Double Gloucester. Made in the English county of Gloucestershire, in the region called the Cotswolds, Double Gloucester was originally made from the milk of the local black cattle of the same name. A firm cheese, Cotswold is blended with chives and onions and aged for three to four months.

INGREDIENTS

2 gallons (7.6 L) whole milk

4 tablespoons (60 ml) mesophilic mother culture, or 1/4 teaspoon (about 2 ml) direct-set culture

4 drops annatto coloring diluted in 1/4 cup (60 ml) cool, unchlorinated water

1/8 teaspoon (about 1 ml) calcium chloride diluted in 1/4 cup (60 ml) cool, unchlorinated water (see page 72)

3/4 teaspoon (about 4 g) liquid rennet, or 1/4 tablet dry rennet diluted in 1/4 cup (60 ml) cool, unchlorinated water

2 teaspoons (about 5 g) dried chives

2 teaspoons (about 5 g) dried onion

TECHNIQUES

For illustrated steps and tools, see Intermediate Cheese-Making Techniques, page 82.

PROCEDURE

Heat the milk to 90°F (32°C), then gently stir in the starter culture and cover. Let the milk ripen for forty-five minutes. Add the annatto coloring, stirring to distribute evenly. If you are using homogenized milk, add calcium chloride.

Maintaining the target temperature of 90°F (32°C), add the diluted rennet, and stir for one minute. Cover and let it set for forty-five minutes. Use your finger or a knife to check for a clean break (see page 83), and use a curd knife to cut through the curds.

Cut the curds into 1/4" (6 mm) cubes. Maintaining the target temperature, stir the curds for twenty minutes. Gradually raise the temperature of the cheese to 104°F (40°C). This should take about thirty-five minutes. Stir frequently to keep the curds from matting. Once the target temperature is reached, maintain for thirty minutes, stirring continually. Let the curds rest for five minutes in the water bath.

Line a colander with sterilized cheese cloth, and rest the colander in a deep bowl. Pour the curds into the colander and drain for several minutes, until the whey no longer drains freely. Pour the curds into a 2-pound (900 g) cheese-cloth-lined mold. Cover one corner of the curds with cheese cloth, top with a follower, and press at ten pounds for fifteen minutes. Remove

Cotswold, a traditional English cheese, has a firm texture and is flavored with chives and onions.

the cheese from the press, and slowly unwrap it. Turn it over, rewrap with the cheese cloth, and press at thirty pounds for ten minutes. Repeat this procedure, pressing at forty pounds for two hours. Repeat again, pressing at fifty pounds for twenty-four hours.

Remove the cheese from the press and take it out of mold. Unwrap the cheese cloth, and place the cheese on a board. Let it air-dry at room temperature, turning twice daily until it is dry to the touch (usually within two to five days). Wax the cheese if desired, or allow the cheese to form a natural rind, brushing frequently to remove any unwanted mold. Ripen in a refrigerator for one to three months at 55° F (13°C) and 80–85 percent humidity. Turn weekly.

Yield: 2 pounds (900 g)

Cantal is often called the oldest of French cheeses due to the fact that historical references date back 2,000 years to Ancient Rome. This cheese is named for the Cantal Mountains in the Auvergne region of France, a rugged area that is blessed with fertile land and a rich cheese-making tradition. Cantal is sometimes called the French Cheddar, because it shares some similar flavor characteristics; it is sweet and light when young, and vigorous and earthy when aged. Unlike Cheddar, however, it lacks some of the tangy acidic notes.

INGREDIENTS

2 gallons (7.6 L) whole milk

4 tablespoons (60 ml) mesophilic mother culture, or ¼ teaspoon (about 2 ml) direct-set culture

⅛ teaspoon (about 1 ml) calcium chloride diluted in ¼ cup (60 ml) cool, unchlorinated water (see page 72)

¾ teaspoon (about 4 g) liquid rennet, or ¼ tablet dry rennet diluted in ¼ cup (60 ml) cool, unchlorinated water

2 tablespoons (36 g) cheese salt

TECHNIQUES

For illustrated steps and tools, see Intermediate Cheese-Making Techniques, page 82.

PROCEDURE

Heat the milk to 90ºF (32ºC), then gently stir in the starter culture and cover. Let the milk ripen for forty-five minutes. If you are using homogenized milk, add calcium chloride. Keeping the milk at 90ºF (32ºC), add the diluted rennet, and gently stir for one minute. Cover and let it set for forty minutes or until a clean break (see page 83). Use a curd knife to cut through the curds and check for a clean break.

Cut the curds into ¼" (6 mm) cubes, and stir for twenty minutes to keep the curds from matting.

Line a colander with cheese cloth or butter muslin, rest it on top of your drain bowl, and pour the curds into the colander. Drain for twenty minutes, making sure that enough whey remains to keep the curds moist. Pour the curds back into the cooking pot and add the cheese salt. Using your hands, blend well and break apart any large clumps that have formed. Let rest in the pot for ten minutes in the water bath to maintain the target temperature.

What Can Go Wrong

Look at this ugly thing! But, as the saying goes, you can't judge a book by its cover—believe it or not, this cheese is still salvageable. So what happened? Quite simply, the mold took over the surface of this cheese, and had itself a field day. To restore this cheese, begin cleaning its surface by scrubbing with a nylon bristle brush that is rinsed continuously in brine solution. Once this is done, be diligent about washing down the cheese at least once a week. Next, clean out any ambient mold in your cave by washing down its walls with brine solution. Finally, make sure that you have a fan running in the cave, as mold thrives in still air. If this problem continues, then the humidity in the cave is too high. The humidity can be reduced by opening the door to the cave for ten minutes every day.

Fill a cheese cloth–lined mold with curds. Have your catch bowl in place, because there will be a lot of whey in the curds. Cover a corner of the curds with the cheese cloth, and press at twenty pounds for thirty minutes. Remove the cheese from the press, keeping it wrapped in cheese cloth, and let it sit on a cheese board at room temperature for eight hours. This step is unique to Cantal and allows for the lactic acid to build up, giving the cheese its unique rich flavor. After eight hours, mill the curds into 1/4" (6 mm) pieces. Return the curds to the mold, and press at forty pounds for two hours. Remove the cheese from the mold and cheese cloth, turn it over, and rewrap with the cheese cloth. Press at fifty pounds for twenty-four hours.

Take the cheese out of the mold and unwrap it. Allow the cheese to air-dry on a wooden board for several days, turning every four hours. When the cheese is dry to the touch, it is ready for ripening. Ripen in a refrigerator at 45°F to 55°F (7°C–13°C) at 80–85 percent humidity for three to six months. Turn the cheese over and wash it daily with a mild salt solution of 2 tablespoons (36 g) salt dissolved in 1 1/2 cups (360 ml) water.

Yield: 2 pounds (900 g)

Artisan Advice

Typically, the cheese known as Chantal comes in three sizes and is named accordingly. Cantal weighs eighty-eight pounds (40 kg), Petit Cantal weighs forty-four pounds (20 kg), and Cantalet weighs in at twenty-two pounds (10 kg). For the home cheese maker I modified the recipe, reducing the size down to a two-pound (900 g) round. For a more dramatic presentation, and a better-looking cheese, double the recipe.

Halloumi

Halloumi is traditionally made with goat's or sheep's milk, with the addition of mint. When using cow's milk, you can add lipase to give it some of the tangy flavor associated with goat's and sheep's milk. A versatile cheese, Halloumi is best known as a grilling cheese, though it can also be broiled and served with fresh lemon.

INGREDIENTS

2 gallons (7.6 L) whole milk

4 tablespoons (60 ml) mesophilic mother culture, or 1/4 teaspoon (about 2 ml) mesophilic direct-set culture

1/8 teaspoon (about 1 ml) calcium chloride diluted in 1/4 cup (60 ml) cool, unchlorinated water (see page 72)

1/2 teaspoon (about 3 ml) liquid rennet, or 1/4 tablet dry rennet diluted in 1/4 cup (60 ml) cool, unchlorinated water

1/2 cup (145 g) cheese salt

Brine solution (see page 86)

1 teaspoon (about 1 g) dried mint, rehydrated in 1/2 cup (120 ml) boiling water

TECHNIQUES

For illustrated steps and tools, see Intermediate Cheese-Making Techniques, page 82.

PROCEDURE

Heat the milk in a double boiler to 86°F (31°C), then add the starter culture and blend for two minutes.

Maintaining the target temperature of 86°F (31°C), add the rennet, stir for one minute, and let rest for forty minutes, or until a clean break (see page 83). To test for a clean break, use a curd knife to make one cut through the curds.

Cut curds into 1/2" (about 1 cm) cubes, trying to keep them as uniform as possible.

Slowly heat curds to 104° F (40°C); this should take forty-five minutes. Continually stir the curds to keep them from matting. Once the curds reach target temperature, maintain the curds at that temperature for an additional twenty minutes while continuing to stir.

Drain the whey off curds into a cheese cloth–lined colander that is set in a catch bowl. Reserve the whey.

Traditionally made from the milk of sheep, Halloumi has its roots on the island of Cyprus.

Blend mint into the drained curds with a spoon. Pour the curds into a 2-pound (900 g) cheese cloth–lined mold. Fold a corner of the cheese cloth over the curds, and press at thirty pounds for one hour. Remove the cheese from the mold, and unwrap the cheese cloth. Turn over the cheese, and rewrap it with the cheese cloth. Press at forty pounds for one hour. The cheese should be firm with a spongy consistency.

Heat the reserved whey in a pan to 190°F (88°C). Take the cheese out of the mold, and cut it into 2" (5 cm) -thick strips. Put the strips into the heated whey, maintaining the target temperature for one hour.

The cheese should have a thick consistency. Drain it into the cheese cloth–lined colander, and let it rest at room temperature for twenty minutes.

Coat the cheese with ½ cup (145 g) of cheese salt, and let it rest for two hours at room temperature.

Yield: 2 pounds (900 g)

Artisan Advice As you prepare for cheese making, leave your milk out of refrigeration for several hours. This will allow you to heat the milk to the proper temperature relatively quickly, saving you some time and effort.

Pyrenees

This is a cow's-milk variety of the more famous Ossau-Iraty, from the southwest of France. This cheese is typically produced in large-scale industrial factories and has a mild flavor due to the young age of the cheese. Traditionally coated in a black wax, it is a simple cheese to make and has a wide appeal. (This version is not waxed.)

INGREDIENTS

2 gallons (7.6 L) whole milk

1/2 rennet tablet or 1/4 teaspoon (about 2 ml) liquid rennet dissolved in 1/4 cup (60 ml) of cool water

1/4 teaspoon (about 2 g) calcium chloride diluted in 1/4 cup (60 ml) cool water

4 tablespoons (60 ml) mesophilic mother culture, or 1/4 teaspoon (about 2 ml) mesophilic direct-set culture

1 tablespoon (18 g) cheese salt

TECHNIQUES

For illustrated steps and tools, see Intermediate Cheese-Making Techniques, page 82.

PROCEDURE

In a stainless-steel or coated enamel pot, heat milk to 90°F (32°C). Add the starter culture, stir, and maintain the target temperature for forty-five minutes. Add diluted calcium chloride and stir for one minute.

Add the rennet to the milk, and stir gently from top to bottom to ensure an even distribution. Cover and set aside for forty-five minutes. You will notice a firm curd set. Use your finger or a knife to check for a clean break (see page 83). Using a curd knife, cut curd into 1/2" (about 1 cm) cubes.

Place the pot in a hot-water bath, and slowly raise the temperature to 100°F (38°C). This should be done over a thirty-minute period. You will notice that the whey will rise to the surface at a greater rate as the curds continue to shrink.

Once the target temperature has been reached, cover for five more minutes, then pour the curds into a colander lined with cheese cloth or butter muslin, with a catch bowl underneath. Tie up the curds into a ball, and let them hang from a wooden spoon resting on the edges of a stock pot to drain for one hour. You will notice a considerable amount of whey draining from the curds initially. After an hour, the ball will be firm and moist but not hard.

Empty the curds into a large bowl, and crumble with your hands. The pieces should be the size of marbles. Sprinkle curds evenly with salt, and distribute the salt throughout the curds with your fingers.

Line your cheese mold with a sterilized piece of cheese cloth or butter muslin. Pack your curds into the mold; this will take a little effort, because you will have to push them in to fit into the mold. Neatly fold the cloth over the top of the curds. Begin applying pressure to the cheese. It is best to start with a light press: five pounds for thirty minutes. Remove the cheese from the mold and cheese cloth. Turn the cheese, rewrap cheese, and press at ten pounds for fifteen minutes. Repeat this process, and press at twenty pounds for twelve hours. Turn again and repeat at the same pressure for an additional twelve hours.

Take the cheese out of the press, remove the cheese cloth, and let it air-dry on a wooden cheese board. This will take anywhere from three to five days, depending on the time of year and heat and humidity of your house. Be sure to turn the cheese a few times each day so that it dries evenly.

Once your cheese has developed a firm rind, ripen at 55°F (13°C), and 80–85 percent humidity, from four to six months.

Yield: 2 pounds (900 g)

Variation: Pyrenees with Green Peppercorns

Follow the directions provided, with the following modifications.

ADDITIONAL INGREDIENTS
1 tablespoon (5 g) green peppercorns
1/2 cup (120 ml) water

PROCEDURE Boil the peppercorns in water for fifteen minutes. Strain the peppercorns and set the water aside. Heat the milk, and add the peppercorn water before adding the starter culture. Add the peppercorns when you are blending the salt into the curds.

Feta

The original Feta was a sheep's-milk cheese that is often associated with Greece. There is some dispute to this claim, as Bulgarians will state that theirs is the country of origin. Whoever is correct in this debate is uncertain. What is known, however, is that the word Feta is actually Italian in origin, derived from the word fette, meaning "a slice of food," and modern Feta is made with goat's milk.

INGREDIENTS

1 gallon (3.8 L) goat's milk

1/4 teaspoon (about 2 g) lipase powder diluted in 1/4 cup (60 ml) cool water

4 tablespoons (60 ml) mesophilic mother culture, or 1/4 teaspoon (about 2 ml) mesophilic direct-set culture

1/2 teaspoon (about 3 ml) liquid rennet or 1/4 tablet dry rennet tablet dissolved in 1/4 cup (60 ml) cool, unchlorinated water

1/4 teaspoon (about 2 g) calcium chloride diluted in 1/4 cup (60 ml) cool water

TECHNIQUES

For illustrated steps and tools, see Intermediate Cheese-Making Techniques, page 82.

PROCEDURE

Blend the milk and diluted lipase, and heat to 86°F (30°C). Add the starter culture, stir, and cover for one hour.

Maintaining the target temperature of 86°F (30°C), add the diluted rennet and stir for one minute. Cover and let sit for one hour, maintaining target temperature. Using a curd knife, make one cut to check for a clean break (see page 83).

Cut the curds into 1/2" (about 1 cm) cubes. Allow the curds to rest for ten minutes at target temperature.

Stir the curds for twenty minutes. Pour the curds into a cheese cloth–lined colander with a catch bowl underneath, and tie into a ball.

Slip the handle of a wooden spoon through the knot, and suspend the bundle over a stock pot for four hours, or until the curds have drained. The drained curds should be spongy, but firm.

Remove curds from the cheese cloth, and cut into 1" (2.5 cm) -thick blocks. Lightly sprinkle feta blocks with salt. Place in a covered container and ripen in a refrigerator for four days at 58°F (15°C) and 80–85 percent humidity. Feta will keep in the refrigerator for up to one week.

Yield: 1 pound (450 g)

Goat's milk gives feta cheese its characteristic tangy flavor.

Caerphilly

This mild yet tangy, cow's-milk cheese has a moist, semifirm texture and is generally sold in cylinders or blocks. It's best eaten fresh (the English prefer it only a few weeks old) and is delicious with dark breads and ale. One of the unique advantages to making Caerphilly is that it has a short ripening period—only three weeks—so you don't have to wait too long to try out your cheese.

INGREDIENTS

2 gallons (7.6 L) whole milk

4 tablespoons (60 ml) mesophilic mother culture, or 1/4 teaspoon (about 2 ml) mesophilic direct-set culture

1/8 teaspoon (about 1 ml) calcium chloride diluted in 1/4 cup (60 ml) cool water (see page 72)

1/2 teaspoon (about 3 ml) liquid rennet diluted in 1/4 cup (60 ml) cool water

2 tablespoons (36 g) cheese salt

TECHNIQUES

For illustrated steps and tools, see Intermediate Cheese-Making Techniques, page 82.

PROCEDURE

Heat milk to 90°F (32°C) in a double boiler, then add the starter culture and stir for one minute. Cover and let rest for thirty minutes at room target temperature.

Maintaining the temperature of 90°F (32°C), add the rennet to the milk, stir for two minutes, then cover. Let the mixture sit for forty minutes at the target temperature, or until a clean break (see page 83). Make one cut with a curd knife check for a clean cut. Cut the curds into 1/4" (6 mm) cubes, keeping the size as uniform as possible.

Slowly raise the temperature to 92°F (33°C); this should take ten minutes. Hold the curds at the target temperature for forty minutes. Be sure to stir frequently to keep the curds from matting. Let rest at the target temperature for five minutes.

Drain the curds into a cheese cloth–lined colander, and let whey drain into a catch bowl for a few minutes. Cut the curds into 1" (2.5 cm) -thick slabs, and stack on top of one another. Turn the stack over, top to bottom, two times in ten minutes.

Though now produced in England, Caerphilly, a mild, cow's milk cheese, gets its name from the village in Wales where it was first made; it was the traditional lunch of Welsh miners.

Using your hands, break the curds into thumbnail-sized pieces, and blend with salt.

Fill a cheese cloth–lined 2-pound (900 g) mold with the salted curds. Cover the curds with one corner of the cheese cloth, and press at ten pounds for ten minutes. Remove the cheese from the press, take it out of the mold, and unwrap the cheese cloth. Turn the cheese, and put a layer of salt on both top and bottom before rewrapping with cheese cloth. Press at ten pounds for ten minutes. Repeat the same procedure, pressing at fifteen pounds for twenty minutes. Repeat the same procedure, pressing at fifteen pounds for sixteen hours.

Take the cheese out of the mold, and let it air-dry. This should take several days. Be sure to turn the cheese several times daily to ensure even drying. When the cheese is dry to the touch, it is ready to be ripened. Ripen in your refrigerator at 55°F (13°C) at 80–85 percent humidity for three weeks, turning several times a week.

Yield: 2 pounds (900 g)

Artisan Advice Although the process of making cheese is not terribly difficult, it can be time consuming. Taking into account all of the factors involved in culturing, renneting, scalding, stirring, milling, and pressing, you should allow anywhere from three to four hours per session.

Cloth-Banded Cheddar

This cheese is not something you can make in a hurry, but you will find it quite rewarding. It has a texture that is drier, with a crumbly flake that is associated with traditional English cheeses. Age it for six months (if you can hold out that long), and see what flavor intensity has developed.

We associate Cheddar with the firm, somewhat sharp yellow English cheese, but the word cheddar also refers to a unique method of layering the curds when making this famous cheese.

INGREDIENTS

2 gallons (7.6 L) whole milk

4 tablespoons (60 ml) mesophilic mother culture, or 1/4 teaspoon (about 2 ml) mesophilic direct-set culture

1/8 teaspoon (about 1 ml) calcium chloride diluted in 1/4 cup (60 ml) cool water (see page 72)

1 teaspoon (5 ml) liquid rennet diluted in 1/4 cup (60 ml) cool water

2 tablespoons (36 g) cheese salt

TECHNIQUES

For illustrated steps and tools, see Intermediate Cheese-Making Techniques, page 82.

PROCEDURE

Heat the milk to 86°F (30°C), then stir in the starter culture, cover, and ripen for forty-five minutes. Add calcium chloride. Maintaining the target temperature of 86°F (30°C), add the rennet to the milk, and stir for one minute. Cover and let it sit at target temperature for forty minutes, or until you get a clean break (see page 83). Make one cut with a curd knife to test for a clean break.

Maintaining the target temperature, cut the curds into 1/4" (6 mm) cubes, and let them rest for five minutes. Slowly heat the curds to 100°F (38°C), stirring occasionally to prevent the curds from matting. This should take thirty minutes. Once you reach the target temperature, hold for an additional thirty minutes, continuing to stir. Let the curds rest for twenty minutes at the target temperature.

Drain the curds into a cheese cloth–lined colander and let them sit for fifteen minutes at room temperature. You now have a large block of curd. Cut the block into 1/2" (about 1 cm) -thick strips, and lay them in an 8" x 8" (20 x 20 cm) pan in a crisscross pattern. Cover with a kitchen towel, and put the cake pan into a sink filled with 100°F (38°C) water, to a depth that comes just to the top of the pan. Make certain that the water does not get into the pan. Keep the curds at 100°F (38°C). Rotate the curds top to bottom every fifteen minutes for two hours. Be sure to drain the whey

Banding Cheese

Cloth banding is the traditional way to form a rind on Cheddar cheese. The advantage to cloth is that the cheese can breathe more effectively than when covered in wax, and proper breathing gives the cheese a richer, fuller flavor. Cloth banding is easy to do, and it gives your cheese an authentic look.

PROCEDURE Place the cheese on a clean sheet of cheese cloth, trace the top and bottom of the cheese, and cut out four circles that are each wide enough for the cheese cloth to cover the sides of the cheese. Rub a thin coat of vegetable shortening on the cheese, covering the entire cheese. Lay the cheese cloth on the top and bottom of the cheese, adhering to the shortening. Repeat the process, layering a second coat of shortening between the two layers of cloth. Cover with the second layer of cheese cloth, and rub the fabric smooth to form a solid seal. Ripen at 55° F (13°C) for three to six months at 80–85 percent humidity, turning weekly.

from the cake pan every time you flip the curds. By the end of two hours, your strips should be smaller and tough, with a smooth, shiny finish on the sides. Tear your curds into ½" (about 1 cm) pieces, and put them back into the pan. Cover and let them sit in the 100°F (38°C) water for an additional thirty minutes. Stir the curds frequently to keep them from matting. Blend in the salt by hand, and let the curds rest for five minutes at room temperature.

Pour the curds into a 2-pound (900 g), cheese cloth–lined mold. (If you are using the Wheeler cheese press you will not be able to fit all of the curds into the mold, unless you use the stainless-steel mold to catch the additional curds.) Press at ten pounds for fifteen minutes. Take the cheese out of mold, and peel off the cheese cloth. Turn the cheese over, rewrap it in the cheese cloth, and press at forty pounds for twelve hours. Repeat this procedure, and press at fifty pounds for twenty-four hours.

Take the cheese out of the mold, and let it air-dry on a cheese board for two to three days. Turn the cheese several times daily to allow for even drying.

Yield: 2 pounds (900 g)

Artisan Advice

The process of cheddaring occurs when the cheese maker takes the mass of drained curds, lays them out flat, cuts them into blocks, and then stacks them on top of each other. Over time, the curd blocks will shrink in size and become firm in texture as they continue to lose whey. The end result is a cheese renowned for its flaky texture and pleasantly tangy flavor.

Colby

Colby cheese was developed in Colby, Wisconsin, in 1885, by Joseph F. Steinwand. Colby is similar to Cheddar, but because it is produced through a washed-curd process, it is a softer, moister, and milder cheese. It is often called Colby Longhorn, which is in reference to the long cylindrical molds that are used to form the cheese—not the cow.

Colby cheese is similar in color and texture to Cheddar, but it has a milder flavor and is softer and moister.

INGREDIENTS

2 gallons (7.6 L) whole milk

6 tablespoons (90 ml) mesophilic mother culture, or 1/4 teaspoon (about 2 ml) mesophilic direct-set culture

4 drops annatto coloring diluted in 1/4 cup (60 ml) cool, unchlorinated water

1/8 teaspoon (about 1 ml) calcium chloride diluted in 1/4 cup (60 ml) cool water. (see page 72)

1 teaspoon (5 ml) liquid rennet, or 1/4 tablet dry rennet diluted in 1/4 cup (60 ml) water

2 tablespoons (36 g) cheese salt

TECHNIQUES

For illustrated steps and tools, see Intermediate Cheese-Making Techniques, page 82.

PROCEDURE

Heat the milk to 86°F (30°C), and gently stir in the starter culture. Cover and let the milk ripen at the target temperature for one hour. If using homogenized milk, add the calcium chloride. Add the diluted annatto coloring and stir.

Maintaining the target temperature of 86°F (30°C), add the diluted rennet and stir for one minute. Cover and let sit for forty minutes at target temperature. Check for a clean break (see page 83) with a curd knife (or your finger) and making a test cut through the curds. Cut the curds into 3/8" (1 cm) cubes. Stir and let rest for five minutes at target temperature.

Heat curds slowly to 102°F (39°C); this should take forty minutes. Stir gently and frequently to keep the curds from matting. Once you reach the target temperature, maintain it for an additional thirty minutes, stirring gently. In the meantime, draw a pot of water (6 cups [1.4 L] minimum), and maintain it at 60°F (16°C).

With a sterilized measuring cup, draw off the whey to the level of the curds. Begin adding the water to the curds and stir. Continue adding the water until the temperature of the curds drops to 80°F (27°C). At this point, you should have added about 5 cups (1.2 L) of water. Maintain the temperature for fifteen minutes, stirring frequently to prevent the curds from matting.

Pour the curds into a colander lined with cheese cloth or butter muslin, rest it on top of a catch bowl, and allow to drain for twenty minutes at room temperature. You will notice that the curds become dry and firm. Pour the curds back into the pot, and mill them into ¼" (6 mm) pieces by hand. Blend in the salt.

Pour the curds into a 2-pound (900 g) cheese cloth–lined mold. Cover the curds with one corner of the cheese cloth, and press at twenty pounds for thirty minutes. Remove the cheese from the press, and slowly unwrap the cheese cloth. Turn the cheese, rewrap it in cloth, and press at twenty pounds for thirty minutes. Repeat this procedure, and press at forty pounds for one hour. Repeat again, and press at fifty pounds for twelve hours.

Take the cheese out of the mold, and unwrap the cheese cloth. Allow the cheese to air-dry on a wooden board for several days, turning every four hours. When the cheese is dry to the touch, it is ready for waxing and ripening. Completely cover the cheese in clear wax (see instructions for waxing on page 81).

Age in your refrigerator at 50°F (10°C) at 80–85 percent humidity for two to three months.

Yield: 2 pounds (900 g)

Artisan Advice Certain cheeses, such as the cheeses on pages 107–113 fall into a subcategory of style known as washed curd. At the end of the scalding and stirring steps, whey is removed from the pot and is placed in very hot water, generally between 120°F and 140°F (50°C–60°C). This washing removes the lactose from the curds, which slows down the acidification process and allows the curds to absorb some of the water, giving the cheese a smooth texture.

Gouda

*Gouda derives its name from a town just outside Rotterdam.
Gouda is a washed-curd cheese made with whole milk, and is
molded into the familiar rounded wheels.*

Gouda is a washed-curd cheese made with whole milk that has a rich creamy flavor and consistency.

INGREDIENTS

2 gallons (7.6 L) whole milk

8 ounces (235 ml) mesophilic mother culture, or ¼ teaspoon (about 2 ml) mesophilic direct-set culture

⅛ teaspoon (about 1 ml) calcium chloride diluted in ¼ cup (60 ml) cool water (see page 72)

1 teaspoon (5 ml) liquid rennet, or ¼ rennet tablet diluted in ¼ cup (60 ml) cool, unchlorinated water

6 cups (1.4 L) water at 175°F (79°C)

Brine

Cheese wax

TECHNIQUES

For illustrated steps and tools, see Intermediate Cheese-Making Techniques, page 82.

PROCEDURE

Heat the milk to 90°F (32°C), then gently stir in the starter culture and cover. Let the milk ripen for ten minutes. If using homogenized milk, add the diluted calcium chloride and stir.

Maintaining the target temperature of 90°F (32°C), add the diluted rennet, and stir for one minute. Cover and let sit at the target temperature for one hour. Check for a clean break (see page 83) with a curd knife (or your finger) and making one cut through the curds. Once you have a clean break, cut curds into ½" (about 1 cm) cubes. Stir and let the curds rest for five minutes at target temperature.

With a sanitized measuring cup, draw off one-third of the whey. Gradually add the heated water and stir. Bring the temperature to 92°F (33°C). This will take about 2½ cups (570 ml) of water. Continually stir to keep the curds from matting at the bottom of the pot. Once you reach the target temperature, let the curds rest for ten minutes, stirring occasionally. Drain off the whey to the level of the curds. Stir continuously as you add more of the 175°F (79°C) water until the temperature of the mixture arrives at 100°F (38°C). Maintain this temperature for fifteen minutes, stirring frequently to prevent the curds from matting. Let the curds sit in the pot for thirty minutes, maintaining the target temperature. Strain off the whey using a colander.

Pour the curds into a 2-pound (900 g) cheese cloth–lined mold. Cover the curds with one corner of the cheese cloth, and press at twenty pounds for twenty minutes. Remove the cheese from the press, and slowly unwrap it. Turn the cheese, rewrap it in cheese cloth, and press at twenty pounds for twelve hours. Repeat this procedure, and press at twenty pounds for twelve hours. Remove the cheese from the press, and bathe it in the brine solution for three hours.

Remove the cheese from the brine solution, and pat dry with a paper towel. Ripen in a home cave (dedicated refrigerator) at 50°F (10°C) and 80–85 percent humidity, turning and washing the exterior daily with washing solution (dip a clean cloth into the brine solution). After three weeks, the cheese is ready for waxing (for more information on waxing, see page 81).

After waxing, ripen the cheese for another three months for a medium flavor, or nine months for a more intense, extra-aged flavor. Turn the cheese three times a week to achieve an even distribution of fats and moisture.

Yield: 2 pounds (900 g)

Cumin Gouda

This is a nice twist on the traditional Gouda. The addition of zesty spice makes the cheese a good choice to accompany dark breads and robust beers.

Follow the recipe for Gouda, with the following modifications.

ADDITIONAL INGREDIENTS
1 tablespoon (7 g) cumin seed
1/2 cup (120 ml) water

PROCEDURE Cover the cumin seeds with water and boil, covered, for fifteen minutes. Add additional water as necessary to keep the seeds covered. Strain the seeds, and reserve the flavored water. Allow the water to cool before adding it to the milk. Heat the milk, and then add the starter culture, as directed in the recipe. Once the curds have drained, add the cumin seeds and blend thoroughly.

Gouda with Mustard Seed

Gouda and mustard seed is a natural pairing.

Follow the recipe for Gouda, with the following modifications.

ADDITIONAL INGREDIENTS
2 teaspoons (about 4 g) mustard seed
1/2 cup (120 ml) water

PROCEDURE Cover the mustard seeds with water and boil, covered, for fifteen minutes. Add additional water as necessary to keep the seeds covered. Strain the seeds, and reserve the flavored water. Allow the water to cool before adding to the milk. Heat the milk, and then add the starter culture, as directed in the recipe. Once the curds have drained, add the mustard seeds and blend thoroughly.

Edam

Washed-curd cheeses, such as Edam, tend to be mild and smooth when young but can exhibit a robust flavor when aged for an extended period of time. Edam is made with low-fat milk, is not washed, and is shaped into balls rather than wheels.

Edam's trademark red wax coating and spherical shape make it stand out on any spread.

INGREDIENTS

2 gallons (7.6 L) low-fat milk

8 ounces (235 ml) mesophilic mother culture, or 1/4 teaspoon (about 2 ml) mesophilic direct-set culture

1/8 teaspoon (about 1 ml) calcium chloride diluted in 1/4 cup (60 ml) cool water (see page 72)

1 teaspoon (5 ml) liquid rennet, or 1/4 rennet tablet diluted in 1/4 cup (60 ml) cool, unchlorinated water

6 cups (1.4 L) water at 175°F (79°C)

Brine solution (see page 86)

TECHNIQUES

For illustrated steps and tools, see Intermediate Cheese-Making Techniques, page 82.

PROCEDURE

Heat the milk to 90°F (32°C), then gently stir in the starter culture and cover. Let the milk ripen for ten minutes. If using homogenized milk, add the diluted calcium chloride and stir.

Maintaining the target temperature of 90°F (32°C), add the diluted rennet and stir for one minute. Cover and let set for one hour at target temperature. Check for a clean break (see page 83) with a curd knife (or your finger) and making one cut through the curds. Once you have a clean break, cut the curds into 1/2" (about 1 cm) cubes. Stir the curds gently for thirty minutes. Let the curds rest for five minutes in water bath.

Drain one-third of the whey from the cooking pot. Add 140°F (60°C) water to replace the volume of whey removed, and stir. Bring the curds to a target temperature of 98°F (37°C). Maintaining the target temperature for forty minutes, continually stir the curds to prevent them from matting. Let the curds rest for five minutes at the target temperature. Drain off the additional whey into a cooking pot using a sterilized measuring cup. Heat the whey to 125°F (52°C), and hold it at that temperature.

Pour the curds into a 2-pound (900 g) cheese cloth–lined mold. Cover the curds with one corner of the cheese cloth, and press at twenty pounds

Edam as Cannon Balls?

One of the most unusual uses for Edam was as cannon balls during a naval battle between Brazil and Uruguay during the nineteenth century. Captain Coe, the commander of the Uruguayan vessel, used the load of extra-aged Edam for cannon balls when his vessel ran out of ammunition. After a few missed rounds, the cheese shattered the main mast on the Brazilian ship, and cheese shrapnel killed two sailors. A few more Edam balls tore through the ship's sails, and the Brazilians decided to beat a hasty retreat. Kind of adds some might to the marketing phrase "Behold the power of cheese," doesn't it?

for thirty minutes. Remove the cheese from the mold, and unwrap the cheese cloth. Set the cheese in the heated whey for thirty minutes. Remove the cheese from the whey bath, rewrap it in cheese cloth, and place it back into the mold. Press at sixty pounds for six hours. Remove the cheese from the press, and unwrap the cheese cloth. Turn the cheese, rewrap it in the cheese cloth, and press at sixty pounds for six hours. Remove the cheese from the press, and bathe it in the brine solution for three hours.

Remove the cheese from the brine solution, and pat dry with a paper towel. Ripen the cheese in your home cave (refrigerator) at 50°F (10°C) and 80–85 percent humidity, turning and washing the exterior daily with washing solution (using a cloth dipped in brine solution). Wax the cheese and store in your refrigerator at 50°F (10°C) and 85 percent humidity, aging for three to eight weeks.

Yield: 2 pounds (900 g)

Leiden

Leiden is a variation on Edam. Cumin was a popular spice in the Dutch city of Leiden during the fourteenth century, so it was only natural that it would find its way into the cheese. Cumin seeds draw out the moisture in the cheese as it matures, making it drier.

Follow the recipe for Edam, making the following modifications.

ADDITIONAL INGREDIENTS
1 teaspoon (about 2 g) cumin seed
1 teaspoon (about 2 g) caraway seed

PROCEDURE Add the cumin and caraway seeds to the curds after draining.

Cabra al Vino

This semisoft goat cheese has the rich notes and coloring of the red wine in which it is soaked.

This recipe is based on a cheese from Murcia, Spain. It is a semisoft goat cheese that has been soaked in red wine, giving the rind a deep violet color. Sweet and smooth, it carries a distinctive flavor of both wine and cheese— a perfect combination.

INGREDIENTS

2 gallons (7.6 L) goat's milk

4 tablespoons (60 ml) mesophilic mother culture, or 1/4 teaspoon (about 2 ml) mesophilic direct-set culture

1/8 teaspoon (about 1 ml) calcium chloride diluted in 1/4 cup (60 ml) cool, unchlorinated water per gallon of milk (see page 72)

1 teaspoon (5 ml) liquid rennet, or 1/4 tablet dry rennet, diluted in 1/4 cup (60 ml) cool, unchlorinated water

6 cups (1.5 L) water, heated to 175°F (80°C)

Red wine, enough to entirely bathe cheese, about 1.5 quarts (1.5 L)

TECHNIQUES

For illustrated steps and tools, see Intermediate Cheese-Making Techniques, page 82.

PROCEDURE

Heat the milk to 90°F (32°C), then gently stir in the starter culture and cover. Let the milk ripen for ten minutes. If using homogenized milk, add the diluted calcium chloride and stir. Maintaining the target temperature of 90°F (32°C), add the diluted rennet and stir for one minute. Cover and let sit for one hour at target temperature. Check for a clean break (see page 83) by making one cut with a curd knife (or use your finger). Once you have a clean break, cut the curds into 1/2" (about 1 cm) cubes. Stir, and let the curds rest for five minutes in water bath.

With a sterilized measuring cup, draw off one-third of the whey. Gradually add the heated water, and stir to bring the temperature of the curds to 92°F (33°C). This will take about 2 1/2 cups (570 ml) of heated water. Stir continuously to keep the curds from matting at the bottom of the pot. Once you reach the target temperature, let the curds rest for ten minutes, stirring occasionally. Drain off the whey to the level of the curds using the sterilized measuring cup. Continue adding the 175°F (79°C) water, stirring constantly until the temperature of the curds reaches 100°F (38°C). Maintain the target temperature for fifteen minutes, stirring frequently to prevent the curds from matting. Let the curds sit in the pot for thirty minutes at 100°F (38°C).

Strain off the whey. Pour curds back into the pot, and mill into ¼"
(6 mm) pieces. Blend in the salt.

Pour the curds into a 2-pound (900 g) cheese cloth–lined mold. Cover
the curds with one corner of the cheese cloth, and press at twenty pounds
for twenty minutes. Remove the cheese from the press, and slowly unwrap
the cloth. Turn the cheese, rewrap it in the cloth, and press at twenty
pounds for twelve hours. Repeat this process, and press again at twenty
pounds for twelve hours.

Remove the cheese from the press, and bathe it in a pot containing one
quart (about one liter) of red wine for twenty-four hours. Remove the
cheese, and let it air-dry for six hours, or until it is dry to the touch. Repeat
the wine bath.

Store the cheese in your refrigerator at 50°F (10°C) and 80–85 percent
humidity for three months. Turn the cheese daily for the first two weeks.
Wipe down the cheese with washing solution (a clean cloth dipped into
brine solution).

Yield: 2 pounds (900 g)

Emmental

Emmental is a cheese that is as beautiful as it is tasty.
Although the recipe calls for two gallons (7.6 L)
of milk, you will get a bigger wheel with more holes,
or "eyes," by doubling the recipe.

Swiss cheeses, such as Emmenthal, are ordinarily made in large wheels, but the recipe can be scaled down for home use. Just keep in mind that making the largest wheel that you can will enable the cheese to develop maximum Swiss cheese holes, or eyes.

INGREDIENTS

2 gallons (7.6 L) whole milk

2 tablespoons (30 ml) thermophilic mother culture, or ¼ teaspoon (about 2 ml) thermophilic direct-set culture

1 teaspoon propionic shermanii powder dissolved in ¼ cup (60 ml) 90°F (33°C) milk

½ teaspoon (about 3 ml) liquid rennet or ¼ tablet dry rennet dissolved in ¼ cup (60 ml) cool, unchlorinated water

Brine solution (see page 86)

TECHNIQUES

For illustrated steps and tools, see Intermediate Cheese-Making Techniques, page 82.

PROCEDURE

Heat the milk to 90°F (33°C), then stir in the starter culture. Add the dissolved propionic shermanii to the milk, and stir thoroughly. Cover and let the milk ripen for ten minutes at 90°F (33°C). Maintaining the target temperature of 90°F (33°C), add the diluted rennet, and stir for one minute. Cover and let sit for forty minutes at the target temperature, or until you have a clean break (see page 83). Once you have a clean break, cut the curds into ¼" (6 mm) cubes. Maintaining the target temperature of 90°F (33°C), stir the curds for forty minutes. Use a wire balloon whisk to get the curds into a uniform shape.

Gently raise the temperature to 120°F (49°C). This should take about thirty-five minutes. Stir frequently to keep the curds from matting. Once the target temperature is reached, maintain it for thirty minutes, and continue stirring with the balloon whisk. Use an up-and-down/twisting motion to expel as much whey as possible. Your curds will be very small and will bind together in a small ball in your hand when they are ready. Let the curds rest for five minutes. Pour off the whey.

Pour the curds into a 2-pound (900 g) cheese cloth–lined mold. Cover one corner of the curds with the cheese cloth, top with the follower, and press at ten pounds for fifteen minutes. Remove the cheese from the

⤳ Downsizing Emmental

Emmental comes in huge wheels, weighing in at 180 to 200 pounds (82–91 kg), typically produced commercially in two wheels at a time. Needless to say, it is impossible for the home cheese maker to duplicate this production, so this recipe has been modified. However, the larger the batch, the more likely you will get the look of the Swiss cheese holes, or "eyes" as they are called, you will be better off if you double the recipe.

press, and slowly unwrap the cloth. Turn over the cheese, rewrap it in cloth, and press at fifteen pounds for thirty minutes. Repeat this procedure, pressing at fifteen pounds for two hours. Repeat again, pressing at fifteen pounds for twelve hours. Remove the cheese from the press, and immerse it in the brine solution. Flip over the cheese occasionally, and let it sit in the brine for twelve hours. Keep the cheese at 70°F (21°C).

Remove the cheese from the brine, pat dry, and put on the cheese board. Store the cheese in your refrigerator at 55°F (13°C) and 85 percent humidity for one week. Be sure to turn it and wipe it down daily with washing solution (using a clean cloth dipped in brine). Take the cheese out of the refrigerator, and put it in a warm room, anywhere from 68°F to 75°F (20°C–24°C). Turn the cheese and wipe it daily with brine solution. The cheese will sit out for two to three weeks as the eye formation takes place. You will notice a swelling in the center, and the sides of the cheese will become rounder. Return the cheese to your refrigerator, this time at 45°F (7°C), at 80–85 percent humidity for three months. Turn it and wipe down any surface mold on the cheese using brine solution three times a week.

Yield: 2 pounds (900 g)

Gruyère

Gruyère, which comes from the same district of Switzerland as Emmental, is best known as the key ingredient in fondue. It is also used in quiche, sandwiches, and on its own. It is simply a fantastic, versatile cheese.

A typical commercially produced wheel of Gruyère weighs about eighty pounds (36 kg), so needless to say, we cut this recipe down a bit!

INGREDIENTS

2 gallons (7.6 L) whole milk

2 tablespoons (30 ml) thermophilic mother culture, or 1/4 teaspoon (about 2 ml) thermophilic direct-set culture

1 teaspoon propionic shermanii powder dissolved in 1/4 cup (60 ml) milk

1/2 teaspoon (about 3 ml) liquid rennet, or 1/4 tablet dry rennet dissolved in 1/4 cup (60 ml) cool, unchlorinated water

Brine solution (see page 86)

TECHNIQUES

For illustrated steps and tools, see Intermediate Cheese-Making Techniques, page 82.

PROCEDURE

Heat the milk to 90°F (33°C), then stir in the starter culture. Add the dissolved propionic shermanii to the milk, and stir thoroughly. Cover and let the milk ripen for ten minutes at 90°F (33°C).

Maintaining the target temperature of 90° F (33°C), add the diluted rennet, and stir for one minute. Cover and let it sit for forty minutes, or until you have a clean break (see page 83). Check by making a single cut with a curd knife. Once you have a clean break, cut the curds into 1/3" (8 mm) cubes. Maintaining the target temperature of 90°F (33°C), stir the curds for forty minutes. Use a wire balloon whisk to get the curds into a uniform shape.

Gently raise the temperature to 120°F (49°C). This should take about thirty-five minutes. Stir frequently to keep the curds from matting. Once the target temperature is reached, maintain it for thirty minutes, and continue stirring using your balloon whisk. Stir frequently using an up-and-down/twisting motion to expel as much whey as possible. Your curds will be very small and will bind together in a small ball in your hand when they are ready. Let the curds rest for five minutes at 120°F (49°C).

Pour the curds into a 2-pound (900 g) cheese-cloth-lined mold. Cover one corner of the curds with the cheese cloth, top with the follower, and press at ten pounds for fifteen minutes. Remove the cheese from the

Artisan Advice Although you could say that all cheeses are cooked as the milk is heated, the cheeses in this section have a higher temperature applied to them during the scalding phase, typically 120°F (49°C) or higher. This process will result in a smaller, drier curd with an elastic quality.

press, and slowly unwrap the cloth. Turn the cheese over, rewrap it with the cheese cloth, and press at fifteen pounds for thirty minutes. Repeat this procedure, pressing at thirty pounds for six hours. Repeat again, pressing at fifty pounds for twelve hours.

Remove the cheese from the press, and immerse it in the brine solution. Flip the cheese occasionally, and allow it to sit in the brine for twelve hours.

Remove the cheese from the brine, pat dry, and put it on the cheese board. Store the cheese in your refrigerator at 55°F (13°C) and 85 persent humidity. Be sure to turn the cheese and wipe it down with the brine solution daily for the first two weeks, and once a week after that. Ripen the cheese in your refrigerator for eight months, minimum.

Yield: 2 pounds (900 g)

Parmesan

This is a modification of the famous Parmigiano Reggiano. People are often surprised to discover that it is made with low-fat milk because it has such an intense flavor. The secret lies in the aging, as Grana cheeses are are hard and well-suited to grating. The word grana in Italian means "grains," and refers to the gritty texture of these cheeses. This trademark texture is obtained through a lengthy aging process (a minimum of twelve months), which results in a cheese with a hard, gritty texture. For this recipe we will age the cheese for ten months, to give the cheese a younger, slightly sweeter flavor.

INGREDIENTS

2 gallons (7.6 L) low-fat milk

8 tablespoons (60 ml) thermophilic mother culture, or ¼ teaspoon (about 2 ml) thermophilic direct-set culture

1 teaspoon (5 ml) liquid rennet, or ¼ tablet dry rennet, diluted in ¼ cup (60 ml) cool, unchlorinated water

Brine solution (see page 86)

TECHNIQUES

For illustrated steps and tools, see Intermediate Cheese-Making Techniques, page 82.

PROCEDURE

Heat the milk to 90°F (33°C), then stir in the starter culture. Cover and ripen for thirty minutes. Maintaining the target temperature of 90°F (33°C), add the diluted rennet, and stir for two minutes. Cover and let sit at target temperature for forty minutes, or until you have a clean break (see page 83). Check by making a single cut with a curd knife, or with your finger.

Once you have a clean break, cut the curds into ¼" (6 mm) cubes. Slowly heat milk to 100°F (38°C); this should take twenty-five minutes. Stir frequently with your balloon whisk.

Take the cooking pot out of the double boiler and place it on the stove. Slowly raise the temperature to 125°F (52°C). This should take about fifteen minutes. Stir frequently with an up-and-down/twisting motion to expel as much whey as possible. The curds will have a very small grain size and will be dry to the touch and squeaky when you chew on them to test for doneness. Let the curds rest for five minutes off the heat. Cover the pot with a plate, and drain off the whey, so as to not lose any curds.

Pour the curds into a 2-pound (900 g) cheese cloth–lined mold. Cover one corner of the curds with the cheese cloth, top with the follower, and press at five pounds for fifteen minutes. Remove the cheese from press, and slowly unwrap the cloth. Turn over the cheese, rewrap it in the cloth,

and press at ten pounds for thirty minutes. Repeat this procedure, pressing at fifteen pounds for two hours. Repeat again, pressing at twenty pounds for twelve hours.

Remove the cheese from the mold, and unwrap the cheese cloth. Immerse the cheese in the brine solution. Flip the cheese occasionally, and let it sit in the brine for twenty-four hours, at 70°F (21°C).

Take the cheese out of the brine solution, pat dry, and place on a cheese board. Put the cheese in the refrigerator at 55°F (13°C) and 80–85 percent humidity for ten months. Turn the cheese daily for the first three weeks of aging, and then weekly after that. Remove any mold that forms on the exterior of the cheese with the washing solution (using a clean cloth dipped into the brine solution).

Rub with olive oil after two months to keep the cheese from drying out. Wipe the cheese with olive oil several times over a ripening period of six months to two years.

Yield: 2 pounds (900 g)

With patience, this pungent, crumbly cheese can be all yours at home. The secret to good flavor and texture lies in the aging of this cow's-milk cheese.

Romano

Romano is one of the world's oldest cheeses, dating back to the Roman Empire. The authentic Romano, known as Pecorino Romano, is made with sheep's milk. Considering that the availability of sheep's milk is limited for the average home cheese maker, I suggest using cow's milk and adding the enzyme lipase. This will give the cheese more of the tangy flavor that is associated with Romano. An alternative approach, for a fuller-flavored cheese, is to blend one gallon (3.8 L) of goat's milk with one gallon (3.8 L) of cow's milk.

INGREDIENTS

2 gallons (7.6 L) whole milk

5 ounces (150 ml) prepared thermophilic mother culture, or 1/4 teaspoon (about 2 ml) direct-set culture

1/4 teaspoon (about 2 g) lipase powder dissolved in 1/4 cup (60 ml) cool, unchlorinated water

3/4 teaspoon (about 4 ml) of liquid rennet or 1/4 tablet dried rennet diluted in 1/4 cup (60 ml) cool, unchlorinated water

Brine solution (see page 86)

TECHNIQUES

For illustrated steps and tools, see Intermediate Cheese-Making Techniques, page 82.

PROCEDURE

Heat the milk to 90°F (33°C), then stir in the starter culture. Add the lipase, cover, and let the milk ripen for fifteen minutes.

Maintaining the target temperature of 90°F (33°C), add the diluted rennet, and stir for two minutes. Cover and let it sit at target temperature for forty minutes, or until you have a clean break (see page 83). Once you have a clean break, cut the curds into 1/4" (6 mm) cubes. Let the curds rest for ten minutes maintaining target temperature.

Slowly heat the milk to 115°F (46°C); this should take forty-five minutes. Stir frequently with the whisk. Once you reach the target temperature, maintain it for another forty-five minutes, continuously stirring to keep the curds from matting. Drain the curds through a cheese cloth–lined colander set over a catch bowl.

Pour the curds into a 2-pound (900 g) cheese cloth–lined mold. Cover one corner of the curds with the cheese cloth, top with follower, and press at ten pounds for thirty minutes.

Remove the cheese from press, and slowly unwrap the cloth. Turn over the cheese, rewrap it in the cloth, and press at twenty-five pounds for three hours. Repeat this procedure, pressing at forty pounds for twelve hours. Repeat again, pressing at twenty pounds for twelve hours.

Remove the cheese from the mold, and unwrap the cheese cloth. Immerse the cheese in the brine solution. Flip the cheese occasionally, and let it sit in the brine for twenty-four hours, at 70°F (21°C).

Take the cheese out of the brine solution, pat dry, and place on a cheese board. Put the cheese in the refrigerator at 55°F (13°C) at 80–85 percent humidity for ten months. Turn the cheese daily for the first three weeks of aging, and then weekly after that. Remove any mold that forms on the exterior of the cheese with the washing solution (using a clean cloth dipped into the brine solution).

After one month, rub the cheese with olive oil to keep it from drying out, and again after a week. Repeat again every month.

Yield: 2 pounds (900 g)

Romano cheese is an enduring favorite with Italian meals, and although traditionally made with sheep's milk, you can closely approximate the flavor by adding special enzymes to cow's milk, or by making it from a blend of cow's and goat's milk.

Bra

Bra originated in the town of the same name, located in the mountainous region of Italy known as Piedmont. Originally, farmers added sheep's or goat's milk to supplement the cow's milk.

INGREDIENTS

2 gallons (7.6 L) low-fat milk

8 tablespoons (60 ml) thermophilic mother culture, or ¼ teaspoon (about 2 ml) thermophilic direct-set culture

1 teaspoon (5 ml) liquid rennet, or ¼ tablet dry rennet, diluted in ¼ cup (60 ml) cool, unchlorinated water

Brine solution (see page 86)

TECHNIQUES

For illustrated steps and tools, see Intermediate Cheese-Making Techniques, page 82.

PROCEDURE

Heat the milk to 90°F (33°C), then stir in the starter culture. Cover and ripen for thirty minutes.

Maintaining the target temperature of 90°F (33°C), add the diluted rennet, and stir for two minutes. Cover the pan, and allow it to set for forty minutes at the target temperature, or until you have a clean break (see page 83). Make one cut through the curds with a curd knife to test for a clean break. Once you have a clean break, cut the curds into ¼" (6 mm) cubes.

Slowly heat the milk to 100°F (38°C); this should take thirty minutes. In order to get the curds to the proper size, use a whisk. Stir frequently with the whisk, using an up and down twisting motion.

Pour the curds into a cheese-cloth-lined colander, and quickly transfer from the colander to a 2-pound (900 g) cheese-cloth-lined mold. Cover the curds with a corner of the cheese cloth, and place the follower on top. Press at ten pounds for ten minutes. Remove the cheese from the mold, unwrap the cheese cloth, and use your fingers to break the cheese into small pieces in a bowl. Repack the cheese into the cheese-cloth-lined mold and press again at ten pounds for fifteen minutes. Remove the cheese from the mold, unwrap the cheese cloth, and break into pieces again. Repack, and press at thirty pounds for fifteen minutes. Repeat this procedure, and press at forty pounds for twenty hours. Repeat again, and press at fifty pounds for twenty-four hours.

Remove the cheese from the mold, and unwrap the cheese cloth. Immerse the cheese in the brine solution for twenty-four hours, turning it every six hours.

Take the cheese out of the brine solution, pat dry, and place on a cheese board. Put the cheese in the refrigerator at 55°F (13°C) at 80–85 percent humidity for six months. Turn the cheese daily for the first two weeks of aging, and then weekly after that. Using a clean cloth dipped into brine solution, wash the cheese once a week.

Yield: 2 pounds (900 g)

Master Cheese Maker

GAIL HOLMES, COBB HILL CHEESE

"It takes time to develop a feel for the curds and determining the right moisture content. This comes with practice."

Cobb Hill Cheese is part of a cooperative living arrangement in the Four Corners region near Hartland, Vermont. Cobb Hill Cheese was formed as a way to provide income for the dairy farmers who are part of the community.

Gail Holmes and her partner, Marsha Carmichael, focus on making two varieties of cheese: Four Corners Caerphilly and Ascutney Mountain (which is similar to a Gruyère).

Cobb Hill Farm uses milk from Jersey cows, which is rich, sweet, and high in butter fat. Because the cows are grass fed, there can be considerable variability in milk quality throughout the year. "Starting in May, the cows produce much more milk, and we are forced to make more cheese," Holmes says. "The milk is also more yellow and gold in color, and it makes great cheese."

The cheeses she produces require quite different techniques and present separate challenges for the cheese maker. "Caerphilly, because it has a natural rind, needs the proper humidity and temperature. If it gets below 65 percent humidity (in the cave), it can develop cracks, which then get moldy." As for advice for the home cheese maker, Holmes suggests starting out with making a fresh cheese to understand the basics. She also points out that it takes practice to get the cheeses that you want. "It takes time to develop a feel for the curds and determining the right moisture content. It is also important to get a good understanding of how pH, temperature, and moisture interact. This comes with practice."

Mozzarella

Mozzarella is one of the most popular cheeses in North America, but it is difficult to find one in a store that is as good as it is homemade. Mozzarella, with Provolone, is part of the family of pasta filata cheeses. Pasta filata means to spin threads. These cheeses have their curds heated and kneaded, which gives the cheese plasticity. This kneading process is significant for the preservation of the cheese as it expels most of the whey, making these cheeses better suited for warmer climates.

INGREDIENTS

1 gallon (3.8 L) milk (you can use low-fat or skim, but the flavor is best when made with whole milk)

8 ounces (220 g) thermophilic mother culture, or 1/8 teaspoon (about 1 ml) direct-set thermophilic culture

1/2 teaspoon (about 3 ml) liquid rennet or 1/4 tablet dry rennet dissolved in 1/4 cup (60 ml) cold water

Brine solution (see page 86)

TECHNIQUES

For illustrated steps and tools, see Intermediate Cheese-Making Techniques, page 82.

PROCEDURE

Heat the milk to 90°F (33°C), then add the starter culture. Let the milk ripen for forty-five minutes.

Add the rennet to the milk, and stir for five minutes. Let the milk sit at the target temperature (90°F [33°C]) for one hour. Insert a curd knife, and make one cut through the curds to check for a clean break (see page 83). Once you have a clean break, cut the curds into 1/2" (about 1 cm) cubes.

Reheat the milk to 90°F (33°C), and maintain this temperature for thirty minutes. Next, slowly raise the temperature to 105°F (41°C); this will take thirty minutes. Once you reach the target temperature, allow the curds to cook for another five to ten minutes.

Drain off the whey by pouring the mixture though a cheese cloth–lined colander with a catch bowl underneath. Place the curds into a double boiler; the water in the bottom pot needs to be at a constant 105°F (41°C). You will have to drain off some additional whey periodically as the curds continue to cook. As the curds are heated at the bottom of the double boiler, additional whey will continue to be expelled from the curds. Periodically drain off the whey. Cook the curds at 105°F (41°C) for two to three hours, flipping them occasionally so that they are evenly heated. They will form a paste at the bottom of the pan. After two hours, test the

pH of the curds; it should be in the range of 5.0 to 5.3. If it is not in this range, the curds need to be cooked a little longer.

Once you achieve the proper pH, cut the curd mass into ½" (about 1 cm) cubes, drain off any excess whey, and place the curds into 4 cups (450 ml) of water that is heated to 170°F (77°C). Using wooden spoons, work the curds into balls by pressing them together. Once you have a ball the size you want (typically, about the size of a tangerine), take it out and work it with your hands, stretching the curds apart and folding them over themselves. The curds are going to be hot, so you may want to wear latex or rubber gloves during this step.

You'll want to knead the cheese several times to get a full, soft texture. If you need to, put the cheese back into the water to warm it up so that it can be stretched further. Once you are satisfied with the size, shape, and texture of your cheese, immediately dunk it into cold brine solution. Be certain that your brine solution is cold, because you want to cool off the cheese as fast as possible; the longer the cheese stays warm, the tougher it becomes. Let the cheese soak in the brine solution for one hour. After soaking, it's ready!

Yield: 1 pound (450 g)

Artisan Advice

Traditionally, Mozzarella was made with water buffalo's milk, but most people have never tasted this kind of Mozzarella because almost all the Mozzarella produced in North America is made with cow's milk. Water buffalo's milk has a dense, creamy consistency.

Provolone

Provolone is a Southern Italian cheese that can be thought of as Mozzarella's older brother. There are two versions of Provolone: piccante, which is aged longer and has a sharper bite, and dolce, with a milder flavor. Let the cheese age for four to six months to get the full benefit of the flavor.

INGREDIENTS

1 gallon (3.8 L) whole milk

8 ounces (220 g) thermophilic mother culture, or 1/8 teaspoon (about 1 ml) direct-set thermophilic culture

1/4 teaspoon (about 2 g) lipase powder, dissolved in 1/4 cup (60 ml) cool water

1/2 teaspoon (about 3 ml) liquid rennet, or 1/2 tablet of dry rennet dissolved in 1/4 cup (60 ml) cool, unchlorinated water

Brine solution (see page 86)

TECHNIQUES

For illustrated steps and tools, see Intermediate Cheese-Making Techniques, page 82.

PROCEDURE

Heat the milk to 86°F (30°C), then add the starter culture. Cover and allow the milk to ripen for thirty minutes at the target temperature. Take a pH reading: the pH should be 6.0 to 7.0. When the proper pH level is reached, stir in the lipase, and let it sit for an additional ten minutes at the target temperature.

Stir in the rennet for one minute, and let the milk rest for thirty minutes at the target temperature. Take another pH reading, with a target of 6.5. If the mixture has not reached the 6.5 pH level, check in 10 minute intervals. Test for a clean break, then cut the curds.

Cut the curds into 1/4" (6 mm) cubes, and allow them to rest for ten minutes at the target temperature (86°F [30°C]). Maintaining the target temperature, gently stir the curds for ten minutes. Gently heat the curds to 102°F (39°C); this should take thirty minutes. Continue to stir to keep the curds from matting. Once you reach the target temperature, stir for an additional ten minutes, and then let the curds rest for five minutes, maintaining the target temperature.

Drain off one-third of the whey using a sanitized measuring cup, and take a pH reading. If the whey has a pH of 6.0, let the curds rest for an additional five minutes at 102°F (39°C). If the pH is not 6.0, continue to stir until the proper reading is achieved.

Set a pot of water on the stove, and heat to 170°F (77°C). You will need this to mold the cheese. In addition, you will need a bowl of cool water for the stretching.

Form the curd into one continuous block, and place it in an 8" x 8" (20 x 20 cm) pan. Let the curd sit for ten minutes at room temperature. Cut the cheese block into ½" (about 1 cm)-wide blocks, and stack them on top of each other. Turn the stack every fifteen minutes, and test for a pH reading of 5.0. Continue turning and flipping the blocks of curds until a pH of 5.0 is reached.

Place one small piece of cheese into 170°F (77°C) water for thirty seconds. If it can easily stretch 2" (5 cm) without breaking, the cheese is ready to mold.

Using a wooden spoon, scoop out the balls from the stacks of curd and dip them into hot water. Let them sit in the water for one minute, then remove the curds from the water and place them in a bowl. Stretch the curds with your spoon or with your hands. The curds will be hot, so wear latex or rubber gloves to protect your hands.

Once the balls have achieved a smooth texture and an elastic consistency, immerse them in cool water, keeping them there until you are ready to brine your cheese.

Immerse the cheese in room-temperature brine solution for two hours. Remove the cheese from the brine, pat dry, and tie kitchen twine around the balls. Hang the balls in a cool area or in your refrigerator at 50°F (10°C) at 85 percent humidity for three weeks. If a sharper-flavored cheese is desired, continue to hang at 45°F (7°C) for an additional two to twelve months.

Yield: 1 pound (450 g)

Artisan Advice Reserve the protein-rich, watery whey as it drains from cheese as it is being pressed. If used when fresh, it is the key ingredient in many delicious cheeses, including ricotta, gjetost, and myseost, whose recipes are provided in this chapter.

Ricotta

Ricotta, meaning "recooked" in Italian, is made with whey left over from the process of creating another cheese. While purists insist on using fresh whey only, fresh milk can be added to increase the recipe's yield.

Ricotta is made from whey drained from other cheeses.
In Italian, the word for ricotta means "recooked."

INGREDIENTS

2 gallons (7.6 L) whey (please note that the whey must be fresh—no more than three hours old)

1 quart (0.9 L) whole milk (optional; add milk if a greater yield is desired)

¼ cup (60 ml) vinegar

Salt

TECHNIQUES

For illustrated steps and tools, see Intermediate Cheese-Making Techniques, page 82.

PROCEDURE

Pour the whey into a large pot, and heat it to 200°F (93°C). Add the vinegar, and stir. You will see small curd particles rise to the surface. Ladle the curds into a cheese-cloth-lined colander, and set aside to drain over a catch bowl. When the curds are cool to the touch, tie the corners of the cloth into a ball, wrap the ends around a wooden spoon, and rest the ends of the wooden spoon on the edges of your sink, allowing the curds to drain.

After a few hours the cheese should stop draining, at which time you can salt to taste. Package the cheese in an airtight container and refrigerate. Ricotta will stay fresh for five days in the refrigerator.

Yield: 2 pounds (900 g

Gjetost
and Myseost

*Here is another use for your leftover whey. Deep brown with
pronounced caramel flavors, gjetost is made with goat's milk
whey, whereas myseost is made with cow's milk whey.
These cheeses are very popular in the Scandinavian countries,
where they are often served as a breakfast cheese, melted
on top of toasted bread. Making these cheeses takes time,
so plan ahead; you don't want to find yourself up at four in
the morning finishing up the cheeses.*

INGREDIENTS

1 gallon (3.8 L) fresh whey (not more than two hours old)

1 cup (235 ml) heavy cream

TECHNIQUES

For illustrated steps, see Intermediate Cheese-Making Techniques, page 82.

PROCEDURE

Pour the whey into a large pot. Leave plenty of room at the top to prevent it from boiling over. Add the cream, and slowly bring to a boil. Once at a boil, turn down the heat to a simmer, and skim off the foam that has formed on the top of the pot. Set it aside in a bowl in the refrigerator. Boil down the whey, stirring occasionally so that it does not stick to the bottom of the pan. When the whey has reduced to about 80 percent of its volume, add the reserved foam, and stir. Continue to reduce, whisking to keep the cheese smooth.

Once the mixture has the consistency of fudge, pour it into a metal bowl or pan, and place it into a water bath to cool. Continue to stir in the container to remove any lumps. When it has started to firm up, put it in an airtight container and refrigerate to set. Cool in refrigerator at about 40°F (4°C) and at 90 percent humidity. Gjetost and myseost will stay fresh in the refrigerator for three weeks, and it should be firm enough to slice.

CHAPTER FIVE

Advanced Cheese Making: The Mold- and Bacteria- Ripened Cheeses

The cheeses in this chapter present a unique set of circumstances that will challenge the basic cheese maker. Although many of these techniques are similar to those in the previous chapter, they do have some additional twists because of the precarious nature of the ripening process. That said, some of the world's greatest cheeses are mold- and bacteria-ripened cheeses, and it is well worth the effort of making them yourself.

Mastering the art of making mold- and bacteria-ripened cheeses, such as the blue cheese shown here, raises cheese making to an edible art form.

Techniques

Advanced Cheese-Making Techniques

◄ **CULTURING THE MILK** This is the first stage in the cheese-making process, where the starter culture is added to the milk. Also known as acidifying, the procedure entails adding the starter to the milk at the proper temperature and letting the culture grow. It is important to ensure that the milk is at the proper temperature and that the temperature is maintained throughout the process. The best way to do this is to heat the milk in a hot-water bath; the kitchen sink works best. In general, the water needs to be 10° higher than your target temperature, which is called for in the individual recipe.

RENNETING No matter what type of rennet you use (dry or liquid), it needs to be diluted to ensure that it is distributed evenly throughout the milk. Use ¼ cup (60 ml) of cool, unchlorinated water (read the labels of bottled water to be sure it is unchlorinated), and if you are using rennet tablets, they need sit in the water for forty minutes before use. Before adding the rennet, make sure that the milk is at the proper temperature stated in the recipe. Rennet is effective between 68°F and 122°F (20°C–50°C). When adding the rennet to the milk, stir the milk gently, both in circles as well as from top to bottom, for about 1 minute. If you are using raw milk or non-homogenized milk, you will need to top-stir as well. This entails using your spoon and stirring the top half of the pot. In these types of milk, the cream rises to the top, and top-stirring will ensure a full distribution of rennet. Cover

and wait the recommended time, which in most cases is 30 to 40 minutes.

◀ CUTTING THE CURD

Cutting the curd takes place once the rennet has come to a complete set. The process of cutting is simple: You use your curd knife to cut rows ½" (about 1 cm) apart and across the pot. Next, turn your pot 90 degrees, and using the same spacing, cut at right angles to your original cuts. The final cut is trickier, because you are trying to break the curd into cubes. The best approach is to use your knife to cut through half of the pot at a 45-degree angle. Turn the pot 90 degrees again, and finish cutting so that you have cheese pieces shaped roughly like cubes. When you start cutting, you will notice a tremendous release of whey. This contraction of the curd and the release of the whey is called syneresis. It is important to remember that the size of the curds will have an effect on the texture of the cheese. Smaller curds will result in a drier, firmer cheese, whereas larger curds will create a cheese with a smoother, softer texture.

Draining Curds ▶

Spoon curds into a colander lined with cheese cloth, and place a catch bowl underneath. Use a piece of cheese cloth that is large enough to cover the cheese when it has finished draining.

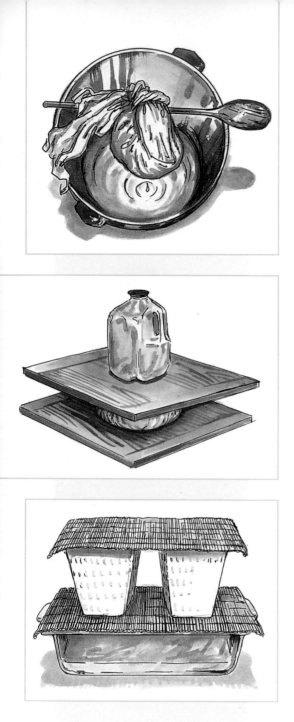

Spoon the cheese curds from the double boiler into the cheese cloth–lined colander, fold the excess cheese cloth over the curds, and allow the whey to drain into the catch bowl for 2 hours.

◄ Draining

Discard the whey from the colander, gather the cheese cloth into a ball, and tie off the ends around the wooden spoon. Let the cheese continue to drain, either refrigerated or at room temperature, according to your recipe instructions—without touching the whey for 8 to 24 hours, as the recipe specifies.

◄ Pressing between Boards

When the whey has stopped draining, place the cheese cloth–wrapped curd mixture on a cheese board. Cover with a second cheese board, and weigh down the cheese by setting a large bottle of water on top. Press the cheese overnight at room temperature.

Salting the Curds

Remove the curds from the cheese cloth, and break them over a bowl into 1" (2.5 cm) pieces. Gently blend salt, as directed in each recipe, into the pieces, taking care not to handle the curds too roughly with your fingers.

◄ Molding and Pressing

Line the cheese molds with cheese cloth, and place them on top of one of the cheese mats. Place the mat on top of the cake pan. Fill the molds with curds, and place another mat on top of the molds. Turn by placing your hands on both the top and bottom of the cheese mats and turning the ensemble over every fifteen minutes for two hours. Continue to turn the cheeses as directed in the recipe you are following; then age the cheese as directed.

◄ Brining

Some advanced cheeses, such as Blue Gouda (see page 142), will need to be soaked in a saltwater solution (2 pounds [about 1 kg] salt to 1 gallon [3.8 L] of water heated to 190°F [88°C]) for a period of time after pressing. Follow the directions in the individual recipes for the length of time to brine the cheese before ripening it.

Aeration for Blueing ►

Sterilize a piercing tool (the stem of a milk thermometer works well) by dipping it into boiling water for a minute. Then, poke twenty holes through the top and through the bottom of the wheel of cheese. Set the cheese on a cheese mat, and place it into your ripening box or bag (see page 150). Cover and put it into your ripening refrigerator at the temperature, humidity, and length of time called for in the recipe.

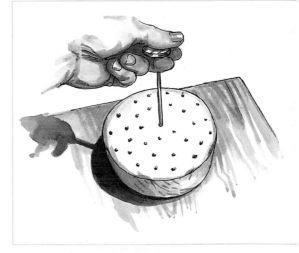

Maturation

Some advanced, natural-rind cheeses need to have their rinds wiped with a piece of cheese cloth dipped into saltwater (2 pounds [about 1 kg] salt to 1 gallon [3.8 L] of water heated to 190°F [88°C]) or sprayed with *B. linens* (see page 170) during maturation in the refrigerator, as directed in the individual recipes.

With the exception of the cheese press, the advanced cheeses require all the same equipment that you use to make the more basic cheeses.

Equipment Needed

Due to the delicate nature of these cheeses, you will need to put away the cheese press (the notable exception is blue Gouda), but you will still need the rest of your equipment. In addition, you will need the following items.

Drying Mats

A drying mat is essential for making mold-ripened cheeses because it provides a breathable barrier that prevents the cheese from collecting moisture on its bottom. You will need two drying mats, sterilized in boiling water for twenty minutes. Plastic or bamboo sushi mats are useful as drying mats.

Ripening Box

All soft-ripened blue and washed-rind cheeses require high humidity, typically in the range of 85 to 95 percent, for proper development. The easiest way to achieve this is to use a ripening box. This is a small plastic box with a tight-fitting lid that can hold the cheese comfortably along with your drying mat. An inexpensive alternative to a ripening box is a freezer-size zip-close plastic bag. Simply put the mat and cheese in the bag, blow the bag full of air, and seal.

Traditionally, straw mats are used for making soft-ripened cheeses, but they are difficult to find. Sushi mats are an excellent substitution, and are widely available. A bamboo mat allows air to circulate around ripening cheeses.

Catch Pan

Soft-ripened cheeses are high-moisture cheeses; consequently, they will expel a lot of whey. The best approach for this is to use a catch pan; often an 8" x 8" (20 x 20 cm) baking pan will do. It is deep enough to capture the whey, and is easily covered with the straw mats.

Cheese Film

Cheese film is a breathable cellophane wrap that will add a protective barrier to your cheese, allowing the mold to bloom (see Resources, page 172). Use this in conjunction with your ripening box.

Carleton Yoder has "always been a foodie." After switching from electrical engineering to food science, Yoder's first job out of school was making hard cider. "During this time I was making cheeses at home as a hobby—everything from blues to Cheddars. In 2003, I left the cider company and went to Shelburne Farms to learn how to make Cheddar. Afterward, I started my own business making cream cheese."

Why did Yoder choose cream cheese over Cheddar? "First, there are many Cheddar makers," Yoder says, "but nobody has been making traditional cream cheese here in New England. Second, there is some immediate satisfaction from making a cream cheese: You add the culture, let it ripen, and then package it."

Yoder loves that cheese making is a blend of art and science. "The scientist in me can take the measurements with my instruments, but then I am also measuring the moisture content by putting my finger into the milk to make an estimate. I love taking a raw product—in this case, milk—and turning it into something new. It is interesting to see the concentration of flavors that come out of something as simple as milk."

Yoder's first and foremost advice for the home cheese maker: "Cleanliness is essential. Ninety percent of all problems with cheese making can be traced to poor sanitation, because it affects the texture as well as the flavor. The other thing to keep in mind is the milk quality. Stay away from the UHT and the ultra-pasteurized milk. I know this may be difficult in the more suburban and urban areas, but if you can find a relationship with a farmer, then you can be assured of getting good-quality milk."

White Stilton

White Stilton, traditionally, was a cheese that used the inferior-quality milk collected during the springtime. It is a young cheese with a very mild, fresh flavor. It is crumbly with lemon-fresh acidity, which is a very different flavor from that of its cousin, blue stilton (see page 140).

INGREDIENTS

2 gallons (7.6 L) whole milk

2 cups (475 ml) light cream

4 tablespoons (60 ml) mesophilic mother culture, or ¼ teaspoon (about 2 ml) mesophilic direct-set culture

¼ teaspoon (about 2 ml) liquid rennet or ¼ tablet dry rennet diluted in ¼ cup (60 ml) cool water

2 tablespoons (36 g) cheese salt

Brine solution (see page 86)

TECHNIQUES

For illustrated steps and tools, see Advanced Cheese-Making Techniques, page 146.

PROCEDURE

In the double boiler, blend the cream and milk, and stir thoroughly. Heat to 86°F (30°C), then gently stir in the starter culture and cover. Let the milk ripen for thirty minutes at the target temperature. Maintaining the target temperature of 86°F (30°C), add the diluted rennet, and stir for one minute. Cover, and let the milk sit for ninety minutes at the target temperature. Check for a clean break (see page 83) by inserting a curd knife and making one cut through the curds.

Line a colander with sterilized cheese cloth, and rest the colander in a deep catch bowl. Using a slotted spoon, ladle the curds into the colander. When finished, the curds should be resting in a pool of whey. Let the mixture sit for ninety minutes at the target temperature of 86° F (30°C).

Tie together the corners of the cheese cloth so that they form a ball. Tie the ends around a wooden spoon, and suspend the ball over a large pot so that the whey can drain freely from the curds. Let the bundle drain for thirty minutes at room temperature. When the whey has stopped draining, place the curd mixture, wrapped in the cheese cloth, on a cheese board. Cover it with a second cheese board, and weigh it down by setting a 1 gallon (3.8 L) bottle of water on the top board. Press the cheese overnight, at 70°F (21°C).

White Stilton with Blueberries

This cheese has a taste that will surprise you. The slightly sweet blueberries blended with the creamy white Stilton make a winner that's perfect for dessert.

Follow the recipe for White Stilton with the following modifications.

ADDITIONAL INGREDIENTS
4 teaspoons (about 20 g) dried blueberries
¼ cup (60 ml) water

ADDITIONAL EQUIPMENT Vegetable steamer

PROCEDURE Using your vegetable steamer, steam the blueberries for fifteen minutes, adding additional water as necessary to keep the steam flowing. Add ¼ cup (60 ml) water to your milk and cream mixture before adding the starter culture. Add the blueberries to the curd before placing it into the mold.

Sterilize a 2 pound (900 g) cheese mold, a cheese board, two cheese drying mats, and cheese cloth. Remove the curds from the cheese cloth, and break them into 1" (2.5 cm) pieces. In a bowl, gently blend the salt into the curds using your fingers. Be careful not to work the curds too roughly.

Line the cheese mold with cheese cloth, and place it on top of one of the drying mats. Place the mat on top of the cheese board. Now gently pour the curds into the mold, and cover it with the second cheese mat. Turn the cheese by placing your hands on both the top and bottom of the cheese mats, and flipping them over. Do this every fifteen minutes for two hours. Then let the cheese sit overnight at an ambient temperature of 70°F (21°C). When the cheese has a firm body, remove it from the mold. Place it on a ripening board and allow it to air dry at room temperature. Place cheese in the ripening refrigerator at 50°F–55°F (10°C–21°C) and 80–85 percent humidity. Turn the cheese four times a day for the next four days.

Turn the cheese three times a week, and clean it off once a week by wiping the rind with a clean cloth dipped into brine solution. Age for four months.

Yield: 2 pounds (900 g)

White Stilton with Candied Ginger

The gentle spice of the ginger goes quite well with the creaminess of this cheese. A little chutney served on the side is a nice accompaniment.

Follow the recipe for White Stilton with the following modifications.

ADDITIONAL INGREDIENTS
1 tablespoon candied ginger, finely chopped
¼ cup (60 ml) water

ADDITIONAL EQUIPMENT Vegetable steamer

PROCEDURE Using your vegetable steamer, steam the ginger for fifteen minutes, adding additional water as necessary to keep the steam flowing. Add water to the milk and cream mixture before adding the starter culture. Add ginger to the curd before placing it into the mold, during the salting process.

Blue Stilton

Stilton, for the English, is a matter of national pride—it is an exceptional cheese. Typically Stilton comes in 16-pound (7.3 kg) cylinders, with a rough natural rind. This mini version has a pleasant balance of blue color and tangy sharpness.

INGREDIENTS

2 gallons (7.6 L) whole milk

2 cups (475 ml) light cream

1/8 teaspoon (about 1 ml) *Penicillium roqueforti*

4 tablespoons (60 ml) mesophilic mother culture, or 1/4 teaspoon mesophilic direct-set culture

1/4 teaspoon (about 2 ml) liquid rennet or 1/4 tablet dry rennet diluted in 1/4 cup (60 ml) cool water

2 tablespoons (36 g) cheese salt

TECHNIQUES

For illustrated steps and tools, see Advanced Cheese-Making Techniques, page 146.

PROCEDURE

Blend the cream and milk in a double boiler. Add *Penicillium roqueforti,* and stir thoroughly. Heat the milk mixture gradually to 86°F (30°C), then gently stir in the starter culture and cover. Let the milk ripen at the target temperature for thirty minutes.

Maintaining the target temperature of 86°F (30°C), add the diluted rennet, and stir for one minute. Cover and let the milk sit for ninety minutes at the target temperature. Check for a clean break (see page 83) by inserting a curd knife and making a single cut through the curds.

Line a colander with sterilized cheese cloth, and rest the colander in a deep catch bowl. Using a slotted spoon, ladle the curds into the colander. When finished, the curds should be resting in a pool of whey. Let the mixture sit for ninety minutes at the target temperature in a water bath.

Tie together the corners of the cheese cloth so that they form a ball. Tie the ends around a wooden spoon, and suspend it over a large pot so that the whey can drain freely from the curds. Let the curds drain for thirty minutes at room temperature. When the whey has stopped draining, place the curd mixture, still inside the cheese cloth, on a cheese board. Cover with a second cheese board, and weigh it down with a 1 gallon (3.8 L) bottle of water. Press the cheese overnight, at 70°F (21°C).

Sterilize a 2-pound (900 g) cheese mold, a cheese board, two drying mats, and cheese cloth. Remove the curds from the cheese cloth, and break them into 1" (2.5 cm) pieces. In a bowl, gently blend the salt into the curds using your fingers. Be careful not to work the curds too roughly.

Line the cheese mold with cheese cloth, and place it on top of one of the drying mats. Place the mat on top of the cheese board. Now gently pour the curds into the mold, and cover it with the second cheese mat. Turn the cheese by placing your hands on both the top and bottom of the cheese mats and flipping it over. Do this every fifteen minutes for two hours. Then let the cheese sit overnight at an ambient temperature of 70°F (21°C).

Turn the cheese four times a day for the next four days, keeping the cheese in the mold. (The molds will make the cheese keep its shape, as it has not been pressed.)

Sterilize your piercing tool, and poke twenty holes through the top and bottom of the cheese. Let the cheese rest on the cheese mat, cover it, and place it in your ripening box at 55°F (13°C) at 90 percent humidity.

Turn the cheese three times a week, and clean it off once a week by wiping it with a clean cloth dipped in brine solution. Age for four months at 55°F (13°C) at 85 percent humidity.

Yield: 2 pounds (900 g)

Blue Gouda

Typically blue cheeses have higher moisture content and looser structure to allow for better mold development. Gouda, because it is a washed-curd cheese, tends to have a tighter structure, which is less advantageous for mold development. However, it will work, giving the cheese a unique flavor and texture.

INGREDIENTS

In addition to the ingredients listed for Gouda, on page 116, you will need:

1/8 teaspoon (about 1 ml) of *Penicillium roqueforti*

TECHNIQUES

For illustrated steps and tools, see Advanced Cheese-Making Techniques, page 146.

PROCEDURE

Follow the Gouda recipe on page 116, adding *Penicillium roqueforti* to the milk before you add the starter culture. After pressing the cheese, pierce it twenty-five times on the top and bottom. Immerse the cheese in brine, and follow the ripening method described in the Gouda recipe.

Yield: 2 pounds (900 g)

Though it's not the cheese we usually envision when we think of blue cheese,
Gouda can take on an additional level of flavoring when treated as a blue cheese.

Camembert

Camembert, so the legend goes, was the creation of a woman named Marie Harel. Marie, a resident of Normandy, France, in 1790, learned the cheese-making process from a priest. However, references to the cheese date as far back as 1569, making a historical cheese, indeed. Making Camembert takes practice and patience, because it requires a higher humidity than most cheeses for proper development.

INGREDIENTS

2 gallons (7.6 L) whole milk

8 tablespoons (120 ml) mesophilic mother culture, or ¼ teaspoon mesophilic direct-set culture

⅛ teaspoon (about 1 ml) *Penicillium candidum*

¼ teaspoon (about 2 ml) liquid rennet, or ¼ tablet dry rennet dissolved in ¼ cup (60 ml) cool water

Cheese salt

TECHNIQUES

For illustrated steps and tools, see Advanced Cheese-Making Techniques, page 146.

PROCEDURE

Heat the milk to 90°F (32°C), then stir in the starter culture and *Penicillium candidum*. Cover, and let the milk ripen for ninety minutes.

Maintaining the target temperature of 90°F (32°C), add the diluted rennet, and stir for two minutes. Cover, and let sit at the target temperature for sixty minutes, or until you have a clean break (see page 83). Insert a curd knife into the curds, and make one cut to test for a clean break. While waiting for the curds to set, sterilize the cheese molds and mats in boiling water.

Once you have a clean break, cut the curds into ½" (about 1 cm) cubes, and gently stir for fifteen minutes, while maintaining target temperature. Let the curds settle for an additional fifteen minutes at target temperature, then drain off the whey to the level of the curds, using a sterilized measuring cup. The mixture will resemble very watery cottage cheese. (*Instructions continue on page 146.*)

The cool, creamy texture and flavor of Camembert cheese can be had by the home cheese maker who has the patience to age it properly.

⤳ Using *Penicillium candidum* to Make Cheese

There are two approaches to using *P. candidum* for making soft-ripened cheese. One is an external application, which is sprayed onto the cheese once when it has formed its shape. However, applying the mold with a spray bottle can be difficult, because it adds more moisture to the cheese, potentially making it too damp for the mold to grow properly. The other approach is to add the mold directly to the milk during the ripening process, thereby inoculating the milk and ensuring that the mold is distributed evenly throughout the milk. Adding the mold directly to the milk is easy, and it works for blue cheese; try it with soft-ripened cheeses as well.

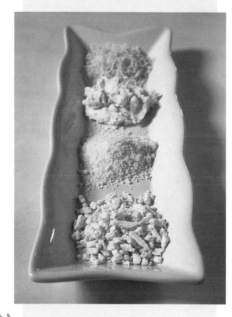

Fat Percentages and Soft-Ripened Cheeses

It is a common question: What does 50 percent, 60 percent, and 70 percent fat mean when it comes to the soft-ripened cheeses, such as Brie and Camembert? This label is concerned with how the French measure fat content in cheese. The French look at fat in cheese as a percentage of the total dry matter, not of the entire cheese. This is known as Percent Maitre Gras.

All cheese contains protein, fat, lactose, and minerals, as well as a certain amount of moisture, based on the recipe. If you were to remove all of the moisture within any given cheese and then measure the amount of fat, you will have the Percent Maitre Gras. Whole-milk cheeses are typically considered to be around 50 percent Maitre Gras; cheeses with added cream can range from 60 to 70 percent Maitre Gras. With soft-ripened cheese, there is a good deal of moisture to the cheese, so the servings of fat per ounce are less than, say, a harder cheese such as aged Gouda.

(*continued from page 144*)

Set one of the cheese mats on top of your drain pan, and place two cheese cloth–lined molds on the mat. Gently ladle the curds into the molds until you reach the top. Once the molds are full, cover each one with a cheese mat. Let the cheese drain for one hour at room temperature. You will notice a dramatic fall in the cheese as the whey is expelled through the sides and bottom.

Now it is time to flip the cheeses. This step is a little tricky so be careful. Work on one cheese mold at a time. Put one hand underneath the bottom mat (you will need to move the mat a little bit so you can get your hand inside the drain pan and underneath the mold), and one on top of the upper mat. Holding the top and bottom tightly, lift them up, and in one quick motion, flip them over and set them back on top of the draining pan. Check to see that the mold is not sticking by gently peeling back the mat, making sure that it does not tear the corners of the cheese.

Flip your cheeses, as described above, every hour for five hours, until they have pulled away from the sides of the molds. Gently pull the mold off the cheese. If the cheese sticks to the mold in places, slide a thin knife between the cheese and the mold to help pry it away. Lightly sprinkle the cheeses with salt, and allow them to rest for ten minutes at room temperature on a cheese board.

Place the cheeses on one of the mats, put both inside your ripening box or bag, and store it in your refrigerator at 45°F (7°C) at 85 percent humidity. After five days you should see a fine film of mold appearing on the surface. Turn over the cheeses, put them back into your ripening box or bag, and place back inside your 45°F (7°C) refrigerator. Continue to age for an additional week to ten days. By now, the cheese should have a good layer of mold on its surface. Take the cheese out of the ripener and wrap it in cheese film. Allow the cheese to continue to mature at 45°F (7°C) for four weeks.

Yield: 2 pounds (900 g)

Fromage Fort

Fromage fort, French for "strong cheese," is a solution to the age-old question of what to do with all of the small pieces of cheese that seem to accumulate in the refrigerator. Traditionally, leftover cheeses would be mixed together and then allowed to ferment in liquid, such as milk or vegetable broth. This version is tamer than the original. Wine or oil is added to stabilize the mixture, and herbs, salt, and more wine are added for seasoning.

INGREDIENTS

1 pound (450 g) miscellaneous cheese pieces at room temperature

¼ cup (60 ml) dry white wine

2 tablespoons (28 g) butter

1 clove garlic, peeled

2 teaspoons (about 1 g) minced fresh herbs (parsley, basil, or sage)

ADDITIONAL EQUIPMENT

Blender

TECHNIQUES

For illustrated steps and tools, see Advanced Cheese-Making Techniques, page 146.

PROCEDURE

Cut all cheese into small cubes. Combine all the ingredients in a blender, and purée. Pour the mixture into an earthen bowl, and let it chill for one hour in the refrigerator, covered. Fromage fort will last for five days in the refrigerator.

Yield: 1 pound (450 g)

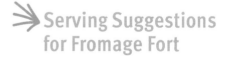

Serving Suggestions for Fromage Fort

Typcially, fromage fort is used as a spread on breads, but its light consistency makes it suitable for topping steamed vegetables, baked potatoes, or any other dish that is enhanced by cheese. As fromage fort is made from any combination of cheeses, its flavor will vary from batch to batch.

Neufchâtel

*There are several varieties of Neufchâtel. The most famous is
Neufchâtel en Bray from Normandy, France, which is the original version.
It is a soft-ripened cheese that comes in a number of shapes, most notably,
in the form of a heart. In North America, Neufchâtel is a term for
low-fat cream cheese, which is nice but not very exciting.*

INGREDIENTS

1 gallon (3.6 L) whole milk

16 tablespoons (240 ml) prepared
mesophilic mother culture, or ¼ teaspoon
(about 2 ml) mesophilic direct-set culture

2 to 3 drops liquid rennet dissolved in ⅓
cup (90 ml) cool water

⅛ teaspoon (about 1 ml) *Penicillium
candidum*

TECHNIQUES

For illustrated steps and tools, see
Advanced Cheese-Making Techniques,
page 146.

PROCEDURE

Heat the milk to 80°F (27°C). Add the starter culture and *Penicillium candidum* and stir. Add 1 teaspoon (5 ml) of the rennet and stir gently. Cover and keep the milk out at room temperature for fifteen to twenty hours.

Once the curds have a firm texture, ladle them into a cheese cloth–lined colander. Tie the cloth into a ball, wrap the ends around a spoon, and hang it to drain over the sink or a stock pot for eight to twelve hours. The cheese should finish dripping its whey and have a firm consistency before you press it.

Place the curd bag back into the colander, and cover it with a plate with a catch bowl underneath. Press with a light weight, such as a 16-ounce (455 g) can of vegetables. Set in your refrigerator to drain for twelve hours. Remove the curds from the cheese cloth, and pour them into molds of the desired shape. When firm, take out and place in a ripening box or bag at 45°F (7°C) at 90 percent humidity. Let the cheese ripen

for seven to ten days, at which point there should be a coating of white mold on the cheese. Remove cheese from the ripening box or bag and wrap it in cheese film or wax paper. Continue ripening for an additional three weeks or until the cheese has a tender give when pressed in the center. The cheese will stay fresh for three to four weeks.

Yield: 1 pounds (450 g)

Traditionally made in a heart-shaped mold, Neufchâtel is a delightfully creamy and spreadable cheese.

Crottin

Crottins (pronounced crow-tan) are small rounds of ripened goat cheese that have a pleasantly fruity flavor. Historical references to this style of cheese date back to the sixteenth century, but not until the early nineteenth century were they referred to by the word Crottin.

INGREDIENTS

1 gallon (2.8 l) goat's milk

1/8 teaspoon (1 ml) direct-set Flora Danica culture

1/8 teaspoon (about 1 ml) *Penicillium candidum*

1 pinch *Geotrichium candidum*

2 to 3 drops of liquid rennet diluted in 5 tablespoons (75 ml) of water

1/8 teaspoon (about 1 g) calcium chloride diluted in 1/4 cup (60 ml) cool water (see page 72)

ADDITIONAL EQUIPMENT

4 crottin molds, sterilized

Straw mats

Catch bowl for whey

TECHNIQUES

For illustrated steps and tools, see Advanced Cheese-Making Techniques, page 146.

PROCEDURE

Warm milk to 72°F (22°C). Add starter to the milk and mix well. Let rest for 20 minutes, maintaining target temperature. Stir in calcium chloride and let rest for 5 minutes. Stir in *Geotrichum candidum* and *Penicillium candidum*. Add the diluted rennet, and stir for 2 minutes. Cover, and keep milk mixture at target temperature; curds will form in eighteen to twenty hours, though it may take up to twenty-four hours for the curds to set.

Check curds for a clean break, and ladle the curds into the Crottin molds, making sure that they are steady as you fill them. Continue to fill the molds as the whey drains off and the curds settle to the bottom. Let the curds drain for twenty-four hours, or until they pull away from the sides of the molds. Place cheeses into the ripening box and store in the ripening cave at 58°F (14°C) at 85 percent humidity. Remove cheeses from the box every other day to remove any excess moisture, and to turn the rounds. They should bloom within two weeks. Continue to ripen to desired flavor.

Yield: 1 pound (450 g)

Crottin, a creamy cheese with an edible rind, is shaped into
petite rounds, from which it derives its name, which
translates as "little dropping." The Crottins pictured above
are commercially made; homemade wheels will be larger,
and less uniformly shaped.

Muenster

The question that often comes up with washed-rind cheeses is, "How can something that smells like that be edible?" Perhaps the question ought to be, "How can something that smells like that taste so good?" Washed-rind cheeses are infamous for their unique aroma, but they represent some of the true gems in the cheese world. Muenster comes from the Alsace region of France, an area with strong German influences.

INGREDIENTS

2 gallons (7.2 L) whole milk

16 tablespoons (240 ml) prepared mesophilic mother culture, or ¼ teaspoon (about 2 ml) mesophilic direct-set culture

½ teaspoon (about 3 ml) liquid rennet, or ½ tablet dry rennet diluted in ¼ cup (60 ml) cool water

Brine solution (see page 86)

½ teaspoon (about 3 g) *B. linens* diluted in cool water

TECHNIQUES

For illustrated steps and tools, see Advanced Cheese-Making Techniques, page 146.

PROCEDURE

Heat the milk to 90°F (33°C), then stir in the starter culture. Mix, and let rest at the target temperature for fifteen minutes. Add the rennet, and stir for one minute. Cover, and let the milk rest at the target temperature for forty minutes, or until you get a clean break (see page 83).

Insert a curd knife, and make one cut through the curds to test for a clean break. Once you have a clean break, cut the curds into ⅜" (1 cm) cubes, and let them rest at the target temperature for five minutes.

Gradually increase the curd temperature to 100°F (38°C) over thirty minutes, stirring to keep the curds from matting. Hold the 100°F (38°C) target temperature for an additional thirty minutes, again stirring to keep the curds from matting. Let the curds rest for five minutes at the target temperature.

Drain off the whey to the level of the curds with a sterilized measuring cup. Ladle the curds into sterilized camembert molds, and place the molds on top of cheese mats. Allow the curds to drain for thirty minutes at room temperature, then flip the molds and mats into a large catch bowl.

Repeat this process every twenty minutes for five turns, then let the cheese stay out of refrigeration for twelve hours on a cheese-drying mat.

Remove the cheese from the molds, and soak it in the brine solution in the refrigerator for twelve hours at 50°F (10°C). Be sure to flip the cheese in the brine to ensure an even coating. After twelve hours, remove the cheese from the brine, and pat dry with a towel.

Put the hydrated *B. linens* in a spray bottle, and using the finest mist setting possible, lightly coat the cheeses. Place the cheese in your ripening box, and store at 60°F (16°C) at 95 percent humidity for two weeks. Wipe down the cheeses with a clean cloth dipped in brine solution every other day. This will encourage the even distribution of *B. linens* throughout the cheese. After two weeks, remove the cheese from the ripening box, and allow it to air-dry at 50°F (10°C) at 95 percent humidity in the refrigerator or ripening cave. Ripen for six weeks, turning daily. Every third day, wipe the cheese down with a damp cloth soaked in brine solution.

Yield: 2 pounds (950 g)

A variation on this cheese is to wash the outside of the cheese with a sweet Gewurztraminer wine instead of the brine solution.

CHAPTER SIX

Butter and Ghee

No discussion of cheese would be complete without the mention of butter. Most people have a love affair with butter, and in a world of hydrogenated oils and fake fats, what could be better than indulging in making your own? There are several types of butter; the two most common types are sweet cream butter and cultured butter.

Once you've made your own fresh, sweet butter, you'll never go back to the store for this simple luxury.

Cultured Butter

Virtually all butter in North America falls under the category of sweet creamed butter. With this type of butter, fresh cream is beaten to remove moisture. Cultured butter is regular butter with mesophilic culture added to it to for additional flavor. This culture provides for a butter that is rich with a full, slightly tangy flavor.

INGREDIENTS

1 quart (0.9 L) heavy cream or whipping cream

2 tablespoons (28 g) of yogurt

1 quart (0.9 L) ice water

Salt

TOOLS

Double boiler

Food processor

Potato masher, or two forks

PROCEDURE

Heat cream to 120°F (49°C) in a double boiler. Stir in the yogurt; cover. Let cream ripen for six hours, making sure the temperature does not drop below 105°F (41°C). Refrigerate overnight.

Heat mixture to 60°F (16°C), and pour it into a food processor, filling less than half way to allow for foaming. Process at high speed. The cream will foam and become more viscous, forming a smooth, then rippled, ring around the blade. When the ring collapses into a slushy mixture of butter particles and buttermilk, stop the machine.

Remove the cover. You will see granules of yellow butter in the white buttermilk. If the mixture appears primarily white, run the processor for a few seconds, until you see real yellow.

Drain off the buttermilk, and add strained ice water in equal volume to the buttermilk removed. Replace the cover, and process for one minute. Drain off the water using a sterilized measuring cup.

If the ice water was cold enough, your butter should be firm, not sticky or greasy. Scrape mixture into a clean, chilled bowl. Using a potato masher or two forks, knead the butter to remove as much water as possible. When no more water can be poured off, salt to taste, and enjoy.

Yield: 1 pound (450 g)

Ghee

Ghee is also known as drawn butter or clarified butter. It is essentially butter with all of the milk solids removed. This makes it ideal for sautéing, because it can stand higher temperatures without burning. Although ghee is typically used in Indian cooking, it has many everyday uses around the kitchen.

Clarified butter, also called ghee in Indian cooking, is ideal for a dipping sauce, and because it has the milk solids removed, it is more heat tolerant than butter.

INGREDIENTS

8 tablespoons (112 g) butter

TOOLS

Heavy-bottomed stainless-steel sauce pan
Skimmer
Colander
Butter muslin

TECHNIQUES

For illustrated steps, see Techniques for Making Fresh, Soft Cheeses, on page 48.

PROCEDURE

Melt the butter over low heat in a heavy-bottomed saucepan. Allow it to foam for four minutes, then remove it from the heat.

Let the butter cool for several minutes. You will notice that the milk solids settle to the bottom of the pan and the butterfat stays on the surface. Use a skimmer to remove the butterfat from the surface, and then pour the liquid through a colander double-lined with butter muslin. Refrigerate when completed.

Ghee can be stored in the refrigerator in an earthenware container, and will stay fresh for about one month.

Yield: 8 tablespoons (112 g)

PART THREE
Beyond Cheese Making

> *"A poet's hope: To be,*
> *Like some valley cheese,*
> *Local, but prized*
> *elsewhere."*
>
> —W. H. AUDEN

Once you have amassed several cheeses in your cave (or your kitchen), it is time to invite your friends to a party. Few foods are as closely associated with entertaining as cheese is, and it is not hard to understand why. It is an attractive food that is flavorful, versatile, and satisfying. (Can you say that about a cheese puff? I think not.) At your next social gathering, I recommend offering an array of cheeses, and implementing some of the serving suggestions found in this chapter.

CHAPTER SEVEN

Serving Your Cheeses

Now that you have a number of cheeses in your home refrigerator, or cave, it's time to invite the family and friends over for a cheese party to celebrate. In this chapter you will find some simple suggestions to make your event a smashing success.

Assembling a Cheese Board

When hosting a cheese party, remember the classic maxim "less is more." You want your cheeses to stand out, not get lost in a crowd. With that in mind, serve only three or four different cheeses at the most. Anything more will overwhelm your guests, and it will be too difficult to appreciate the individual flavors of the cheese varieties.

How Much Cheese to Serve

This depends on your crowd, and what is planned for the evening. The usual suggestion is about one-third of a pound of cheese per person. Bear in mind what kind of entertaining you are planning. If there is a full meal, then this number is about right. If the cheese is to *be* the meal, then you will want to bump it up a bit, putting out enough for a filling portion for each person.

More is less when serving cheese—let your cheese take center stage. Offer white crackers or bread that will not overwhelm the flavor of the cheese.

What Types of Cheese to Serve

Balance is the key. Focus on a blend of different styles of cheese, not simply the same varieties. A good cheese board is like a musical trio or quartet: three or four distinct varieties that come together to create a memorable experience. For example, a good blue cheese, soft-ripened Brie or Camembert, and hearty Cheddar will complement each other.

Serving Suggestions

A cheese wedge that weighs in at about a third of a pound is about the right amount of cheese to allow for one person, so a simple formula for serving any number of people would be to allow one wedge of any type of cheese per person.

Cheeses, like all things, have particular needs. Here are some tips for assembling your selections.

SERVE YOUR CHEESES AT ROOM TEMPERATURE Cheeses taste best when they are at ambient temperature, not right out of the refrigerator or ripening room, because the cold diminishes flavor. Let the cheeses sit out for forty-five minutes to an hour before eating.

DRESS FOR THE PARTY A good cheese board looks the part. Save the plastic cutting board for chopping onions, and go for a good-looking wooden board. The same goes for your knives. Special cheeses deserve special knives. Kitchen knives stay in the kitchen, period!

ACCOMPANIMENTS Breads are usually served with cheeses, and they are a good match. The usual approach is to use simple breads, so that they don't interfere with the flavor of the cheeses. A heavy rye bread, for example, will have too strong a flavor for most cheeses. A good choice is white or whole-wheat bread with dried fruits, which add a nice sweetness to balance the saltiness of the cheeses. As for fruit, acidic types are best. Apples and grapes, for example, are excellent palate cleansers.

Pairing Wine with Cheese

Wine provides a crisp balance to the often full flavors of cheese. When choosing wine, the most important thing to remember is that if you are focusing on cheese, then the wine should play the supporting role. Set aside your Grand Cru Classe Saint-Emilion, and keep your wines simple. A light white, such as a French Chablis, Sancerre, or Graves is a good choice.

The art of pairing wine and cheese provides an endless source of discussion among "foodies." At one time this was not such an issue, as it was rare for cheese and wine to travel beyond their local regions of origin. Choosing which cheese to pair with which wine was as simple as selecting from whatever was available from the local producers.

Rather than suggest specific cheese and wine pairs, I offer some creative guidelines.

- In general, white wines pair better with cheese than red wines. (However, do not keep from experimenting!)

- Together, wine and cheese need counterbalance or foiling (via acidity or tannin), or they require a matched texture and flavor profile. Rich wines should be paired with rich, creamy cheeses, and sharp wines with sharper cheeses.

- The salt in the cheese exaggerates the taste of alcohol in the wine, making it seem "hotter." A salty taste in cheese is best counterbalanced by a hint of sweetness in wine (think Stilton and port, Roquefort and sauternes).

- Stronger-flavored cheeses (such as mature, washed-rind cheeses) are the most difficult to match and do not go well with strong, ample-bodied wines (especially reds). Pungent cheeses are best complemented by sweet wines. Oaky wines clash and overwhelm most cheeses, unless oak flavors are inherently associated with them.

A cheese board should look sumptuous but not have a bewildering selection of cheeses. Clean-tasting, slightly acidic fruits, such as grapes and berries, complement most cheeses and cleanse the palate between bites.

- You aren't compromising aesthetics by switching back to dry white wine for your cheese course. If your cheese course follows a dish accompanied by red wine, and is being served before (or instead of) dessert, the two styles of wine can coexist.

- When in doubt, go native. Local cheese and wines tend to work well together, and can be paired confidently.

- When planning a cheese course, choose either the cheese or the wine first, or pick an array of both that offers a range of possibility for all palates.

- The use of herbs, spices, and crusts in or on the cheese, as they may influence the effect of the wine. Also, don't overlook the potential for incorporating cheese into salads and other light dishes for the complementary flavors offered.

Pairing Beer with Cheese

While matching wine and cheese can be difficult, selecting a beer to pair with cheese is a friendlier affair. As beer is carbonated, it cleanses the palate effectively. Beer has a broad range of flavors, running the gamut from fruity ales to hoppy IPAs, creating a long roster of potential pairs. As with wines, there are some general suggestions you should keep in mind when planning a spread.

- Fresh cheeses pair well with mellow beers, such as American wheat beers, American lagers, and German lagers.

- Soft-ripened cow's-milk cheeses, such as Neufchâtel, Brie, and Camembert, are excellent companions for pilsners, porters, and pale ales.

- Washed-rind cheeses, such as Muenster, are complements to English brown, amber, and Belgian pale ales.

- Semihard cheeses, such as Cheddar, Edam, and Gouda, as well as the cooked-curd cheeses, such as Emmentaler and Gruyère, go well with pilsners, IPAs, double bocks, and Belgian ales.

- Parmesans and Romanos need a heavier beer as a partner: try a strong ale, stout, or porter.

- Because of their intense flavor, blue-vein cheeses require a beer that can hold its own. Try stronger porters, stouts, and heavier dark beers, such as barley wine.

- Goat cheeses are usually a bit more flavorful, so consider pairing them with IPAs, ESBs, brown ales, and porters.

- Pasta filata, particularly Provolone, are well matched with Bavarian whites and heavier Bavarian wheat beers (doppelweizen).

Balance is the key to creating an aesthetically pleasing spread. A good cheese board is like a musical trio or quartet: three or four distinct varieties coming together to create a memorable, edible experience.

Glossary

Acid curd The gelatinous state that milk comes to when a high level of acidity is created through the activity of starter bacteria, or through the induction of acid into the milk from an outside source (i.e., vinegar for paneer).

Acidification The process of increasing the acid level in milk, thereby allowing the solids to come to the surface of the milk.

Aging The final process in cheese making during which the cheese is stored in a specific environment for a specific amount of time in order to develop its flavor and texture. Two important factors involved in aging are temperature and humidity.

Annatto coloring A natural vegetable extract from the seeds of the annatto (*Bixa orellana*) plant found in South America. Annatto is used to add coloring to cheese, giving it the bright yellow often found in Cheddars.

Brevibacterium linens (B. Linens) Bacterium that is applied to the exterior of washed-rind cheeses that aids in the ripening and maturation of the cheese.

Bacteria Omnipresent, microscopic, single-cell organisms. In cheese making there are two major types of bacteria: lactic acid–producing bacteria, which are essential to making virtually all cheeses, and *B.linens*, the ripening bacteria used for the development of washed-rind cheeses such as Limburger and Muenster.

Blue-veined cheeses These are the family of cheeses that rely on the blue mold, *Penicillium roqueforti* for development.

Brine A mixture of noniodized salt and water. Brine serves many functions in cheese making. It acts as preservative inhibiting the growth of surface mold, helps to develop a rind on the cheese, and adds an element of flavor to the cheese.

Calcium chloride A white, powdered salt that is added to homogenized cow's milk or goat's milk to help produce a firm curd structure.

Carotenoids Secondary pigments found in plant matter that are involved in photosynthesis.

Casein This milk protein is one of the key elements giving cheese its structure and body.

Cheddaring The process of stacking and turning curd blocks. This technique applies specifically to Cheddar making. When the whey has drained from the vat, the remaining curd mass is cut into blocks, leaving a drainage channel down the center. These blocks are then turned over. After five to ten minutes the blocks are piled one on top of the other. The process is repeated, inverting the blocks in the vat. The weight of the curd helps to squeeze out the moisture and develop a "chicken breast" texture, which is the ideal Cheddar curd texture.

Cheese press A mechanical device that applies pressure to curds to expel whey. Presses come in many different shapes and sizes.

Cheese starter This is the bacterial culture that is added to milk during the first step of cheese production. The bacteria thrive on the milk sugar (*see* lactose), converting it into lactic acid, which results in an acid curd. There are two types of cheese starters: thermophilic and mesophilic.

Cheese wax A combination of paraffin and microcrystalline wax with a low melting point. When applied to the surface of a cheese, wax will produce an airtight seal.

Cheese salt A coarse, textured salt.

Cheese trier An essential tool used to determine whether a cheese has matured properly.

Coagulation The stage where milk becomes solidified into a solid mass through the action of enzymes (*see* rennet) or acid.

Cooking Heat treatment of curd. The primary function of cooking is to shrink the curd and expel moisture. Cooking reaches a higher temperature than scalding and is often associated with larger-sized cheeses.

Curd A coagulation of milk protein. In cheese making, the curd, created under the influence of rennet, is like a sponge holding whey, fat, other milk solids, and an abundance of acidifying and flavor-producing bacteria.

Curd cutting The process during which the curd is cut into equal-sized pieces, resulting in the release of whey from the curd.

Curd knife A long knife used to cut the curds. Ideally, a curd knife should have a blade long enough to reach to the bottom of the pot without the curds touching the handle

Direct-set cultures Prepared starter cultures that are used to induce lactic acid in milk at the beginning of the cheese-making process. Direct-set cultures are designed to be used only once and do not require any re-culturing, unlike a mother culture.

Drying Dehydration of the cheese surface to help form a rind. This is a crucial part in the manufacture of mold-ripened cheese such as Camembert. Inadequate drying can lead to excessive mold growth and quicker breakdown of the curd than desired.

Dry matter The entire composition of a cheese without moisture; this will include protein, fats, minerals, and lactose.

Geotrichum candidum Another mold that is used for making soft-ripened cheeses. Typically it is the white mold found on the surface of certain smear cheeses, or it is added to Brie or Camembert to aid in the development of the rind. It can be applied either directly to the milk before renneting or sprayed on the surface of the cheese before ripening.

Homogenization The mechanical process of breaking down the size of fat globules in milk so that they will stay suspended in the milk, thereby not rising to the surface. Homogenized milk, though widely available, does present problems for cheese making, and its use requires the addition of calcium chloride.

Lactic acid The acid produced in milk during cheese making. Starter culture bacteria thrive on the lactose; the by-product is lactic acid.

Lactose The naturally occurring sugar found in milk. Lactose composes up to five percent of the total weight of milk.

Maturing The controlled storage of cheese. Different cheeses require different temperature and humidity to mature to their optimum level. Typically, hard cheeses of most types will mature well in a temperature range between 54°F to 57°F (12°C–14°C) and a humidity band of 85–90 percent.

Microbial rennet Yeast or bacteria that contains chymosin (the active ingredient found in animal rennet). Typically it is derived from the mold *Murhor mehi*.

Milk A liquid secreted from the mammary glands of female mammals to nourish their young.

Milling Breaking curds into smaller pieces before putting them into a mold and pressing.

Mesophilic culture Lactic-acid producing starter bacteria that are used to make cheeses at or below 102°F (39°C).

Paste The inside of the cheese.

Pasteurization The heating of milk to destroy pathogenic organisms. For the home cheese maker this is done at 145°F (63°C) for thirty minutes.

Penicillium candidum The white mold that is responsible for the development of soft-ripened cheeses such as Brie and Camembert. The mold is essential to developing the soft, smooth texture, as well as the rich flavor.

Penicillium roqueforti The blue mold that is responsible for the creation of blue cheeses. Its origins lie in the ripening caves in the town of Roquefort in France. Originally, *Penicillium roqueforti* was developed by inoculating rye bread in the caves; today, it is a factory-produced product.

Pressing The application of pressure to the cheese to drive out moisture and fuse the milled curd together. The pressing procedure differs between cheeses, depending on their size and desired texture.

Propionic acid The enzyme that is responsible for the development of eyes in Emmental cheeses.

Raw milk Milk that is taken directly from the animal and has not been pasteurized.

Rennet A coagulant used in cheese making. The active agent in rennet is an enzyme called chymosin. Traditionally, chymosin would be extracted from the fourth stomach of a calf, kid, or lamb. There are various vegetarian rennets that contain chymosin, which has been generated by adapting yeast or mold cultures.

Salting The process of adding salt to the curds. Salt is added to the milled curds before pressing or to the surface of a finished cheese

Soft-ripened cheeses Also known as mold-ripened cheeses, this group of cheeses relies on the induction of specific molds to mature. Brie and Camembert are the most famous of the soft-ripened cheeses.

Ripening The process in cheese making that occurs after the introduction of starter cultures and before renneting. During ripening, the milk is allowed to develop increased acidity from the addition of the cultures and the milk sugars.

Starter culture A preparation of bacteria that, when added to milk, consumes lactose and produces lactic acid. The resulting acidification is one of the techniques used in cheese making.

Thermalization The process of heating milk to 145°F (63°C) for ten to fifteen seconds. This treatment results in less damage to the milk enzymes and non-starter bacteria than full pasteurization, thereby giving the cheese a better flavor.

UHT milk Ultra Heat-Treated (UHT) milk is any milk that is subjected to a few seconds of heating at 275°F to 300°F (140°C–150°C). UHT is popular for its extended shelf life, and because it does not require refrigeration until opened. UHT milk cannot be used for cheese making.

Washing curd Replacing an amount (usually a third) of the whey removed from the vat with water. Washing helps to control acidity by reducing the amount of lactose and bacteria. Cheeses with a rubbery texture are often washed-curd cheeses.

Washed-rind cheese A group of cheeses that are ripened using a heavy growth of the bacterium *B. linens*. These cheeses are called "washed" due to the fact that the bacterium does not spread evenly over the surface of the cheese and must be assisted by washing, typically with a rag soaked in brine solution (but hands will also work). These cheeses have a typically strong aroma and flavor.

Whey The by-product of cheese making. It contains water, lactose (milk sugar), minerals, and albuminous proteins. Whey can be used for making cheese, most notably Ricotta, as well as some cooked cheeses such as myseost.

Index

Index

Resources

Cheese-Making Suppliers

These suppliers will provide you with everything you need to make cheese, with the exception of the milk.

CANADA

Glengarry Cheesemaking and Dairy Supply
21048 Concession #10, RR #2
Alexandria, Ontario K0C 1A0
Canada
888-816-0903
www.glengarrycheesemaking.on.ca

UNITED KINGDOM

Mooreland Cheesemakers
Brewhamfield Farm
North Brewham, Bruton
Somerset BA100QQ
UK
0441749850108
www.cheesemaking.co.uk

UNITED STATES

Dairy Connection
10 Levine Ct.
Madison, WI 53741
USA
608-242-9030
608-242-9036
www.dairyconnection.com

The Grape & Granary
915 Home Ave.
Akron, OH 44310
USA
800-695-9870
www.thegrape.net

Leeners
9293 Olde Eight Rd.
Northfield, OH 44067
USA
800-543-3697
www.Leeners.com

New England Cheese Making Supply
P. O. Box 85
292 Main St.
Ashfield, MA 01330-0085
USA
413-628-3808
413-628-4061
www.cheesemaking.com

Websites with Cheese-Making Information

schmidling.netfirms.com/making.htm
Jack Schmidling's website covers the basics of cheese making; the company is home to the Cheeseypress.

biology.clc.uc.edu/Fankhauser/Cheese/Cheese.html
Frankhauser's quirky cheese page shows every aspect of cheese making, and is complete with photographs. (The homemade cheese press he has constructed it is not to be missed.)

www.foodsci.uoguelph.ca/dairyedu/cheese2.html
Department of Food Science, University of Guelph, Guelph, Ontario, Canada. Packed with technical information as well as cheese recipes and resources.

Source of Artisan Cheeses

South End Formaggio
268 Shawmut Ave.
Boston, MA 02118
USA
617-350-6996
www.southendformaggio.com

Sources for Raw Milk

For those who are interested in purchasing raw, unpasteurized milk for cheese making, here is a summary of the availability at the time this book is being written. This information was made available from A Campaign for Real Milk, an organization dedicated to promoting access to raw milk. You can find out more about this organization by visiting their website www.realmilk.com. There you will find further details and a listing of dairies by state and county.

UNITED KINGDOM

There are reportedly around 200 producers of raw milk in England. This milk is sold directly to the consumer. In Wales, designated farms can legally sell raw milk directly to the consumer.

UNITED STATES

Alabama: Raw milk sales for animal consumption only.

Alaska: Raw milk sales are illegal, but regulations are interpreted to permit raw milk distribution through a cow-share program.

Arizona: Raw milk sales are legal, provided the milk carries a warning label.

Arkansas: Raw milk sales are illegal, with the exception of on-farm sales, directly to the consumer, of raw goat milk.

California: Raw milk sales are legal by licensed farms, and raw milk may be sold on the farm and in retail stores in every county, with the exception of Humboldt. Currently, there are only two producers, due to the additional fees for testing required by the state.

Colorado: Raw milk sales are permitted only through the Guidestone, a cow-share program in Loveland.

Connecticut: Raw milk sales are legal from licensed farms in retail stores and directly on the farm.

Delaware: Raw milk sales are illegal.

District of Columbia: Raw milk sales are illegal.

Florida: Raw milk sales are illegal.

Georgia: Raw milk sales are illegal, with the exception for animal consumption.

Hawaii: Raw milk sales are illegal.

Idaho: Raw milk sales are legal with a license, but there are none currently in operation.

Illinois: Raw milk sales are legal if the product conforms to the state regulations and is sold on the farm. Customers must bring their own containers.

Indiana: Raw milk sales are illegal with the exception of on-farm sales "for pet consumption only."

Iowa: Raw milk sales are illegal.

Kansas: Raw milk sales are legal only if purchased on the farm.

Kentucky: Raw milk sales are illegal, with the exception of the purchase of goat's milk with the written prescription from a licensed physician.

Louisiana: Raw milk sales are illegal.

Maine: Raw milk sales are legal at the retail level and on the farm.

Maryland: Raw milk sales are illegal.

Massachusetts: Raw milk sales are permitted through licensed farms. This is decided on a town-by-town basis.

Michigan: Raw milk sales are illegal.

Minnesota: Raw milk sales are permitted directly on the farm, no permit is required.

Mississippi: Raw milk sales are permitted for on-farm sales of raw goat's milk only. The farm must have no more than nine goats producing milk.

Missouri: Raw milk sales are legal on an on-farm basis.

Montana: Raw milk sales are illegal.

Nebraska: Raw milk sales are legal for on-farm customers. However, the farmer may not legally advertise the sale of raw milk, which includes informing someone on the telephone that he or she sells raw milk.

Nevada: Raw milk sales are legal, but none is available.

New Hampshire: Raw milk sales are permitted on the farm up to twenty-five quarts (24 L) per day; customers must bring their own containers. A milk plant may also sell raw milk directly to the consumer.

New Jersey: Raw milk sales are illegal.

New Mexico: Raw milk sales are legal at retail and on the farm.

New York: Raw milk sales are permitted on the farm only. Currently, seven farms are licensed to sell raw milk.

North Carolina: Raw milk sales are permitted on-farm for animal consumption only.

North Dakota: Raw milk sales are illegal with the exception for pet consumption.

Ohio: Raw milk sales are illegal with the exception of farms who sold raw milk before 1965 when the law was changed. Currently there are no farms selling raw milk.

Oklahoma: Raw milk sales are permitted at the farm; customers must supply their own container.

Oregon: Raw milk sales are permitted for goat's milk on the farm and at retail. Raw cow's milk is permitted only on farms with fewer than three milking cows.

Pennsylvania: Raw milk sales are permitted at retail and at the farm.

Rhode Island: Raw milk sales are illegal with the exception of raw goat's milk from the farm to the consumer with a physician's prescription.

South Carolina: Raw goat's milk is permitted for on-farm purchase and in retail stores. Raw cow's milk is allowed only for farm-direct sales to consumers.

South Dakota: Raw milk purchases are permitted on-farm only.

Tennessee: Raw milk sales are illegal with the exception of pet consumption. A cow-share program is legal.

Texas: Raw milk is legal only as farm-direct to consumers, providing the farm holds a grade A "Raw for retail" license. Currently no cow dairies have this permit, though there are a few goat dairies. There are several cow-share programs active in the state.

Utah: Raw milk sales are permitted on-farm directly to the consumer.

Vermont: Raw milk sales are legal only through on-farm direct to the consumer. Farmers are permitted to sell only twenty-five quarts (24 L) per day.

Virginia: Raw milk sales are illegal. Cow-share programs are available.

Washington: Only certified grade-A dairies can sell raw milk, but none have taken this step since the 1920s. Cow-share programs are widely available.

West Virginia: Raw milk sales are illegal.

Wisconsin: Although the Wisconsin statutes do not prohibit "incidental sales of milk directly to the consumer at the dairy farm where the milk was produced," health inspectors interpret "incidental" as one sale and no more. This has essentially eliminated raw milk purchases.

Wyoming: Raw milk sales are illegal.

Books and Magazines on Cheese and Cheese Making

Androuet, Pierre. *The Complete Encyclopedia of French Cheese.* (Harper's Magazine Press, 1973). This book is out of print, but available through libraries and used-book sellers (including Amazon.com).

Baboin-Jaubert, Alix. *Cheese: Selecting, Tasting and Serving the World's Finest Cheeses.* (Laurel Glenn Publishing, 2003).

Carroll, Ricki. *Home Cheese Making: Recipes for 75 Delicious Cheeses.* (Storey Publishing, 1982).

Caseus International.
This journal is published three times per year, and is full of informative articles on cheese and cheese making. Contact New England Cheese Making Supply (see page 173) for a subscription or back issues.

Jenkins, Steve. *The Cheese Primer.* (Workman Publishing Company, 1996).

McCalman, Max, and David Gibbons. *The Cheese Plate.* (Clarkson Potter, 2002).

Mont-Laurier Benedictine Nuns. *Goat Cheese Small Scale.* (New England Cheesemaking, 1983).

Rance, Patrick. *The French Cheese Book.* (Papermac, 1991).
This book is out of print but can be found through used book sellers (including Amazon.com).

Scott, R. *Cheese Making Practice.* (R. K. Robinson and R. A. Wilbey, 1998).
First printed in 1981 and designed for the industrial cheese maker.

Werlin, Laura, Steven Jenkins, and Martin Jacobs. *The New American Cheese.* (Stewart, Tabori, and Chang, 2000).

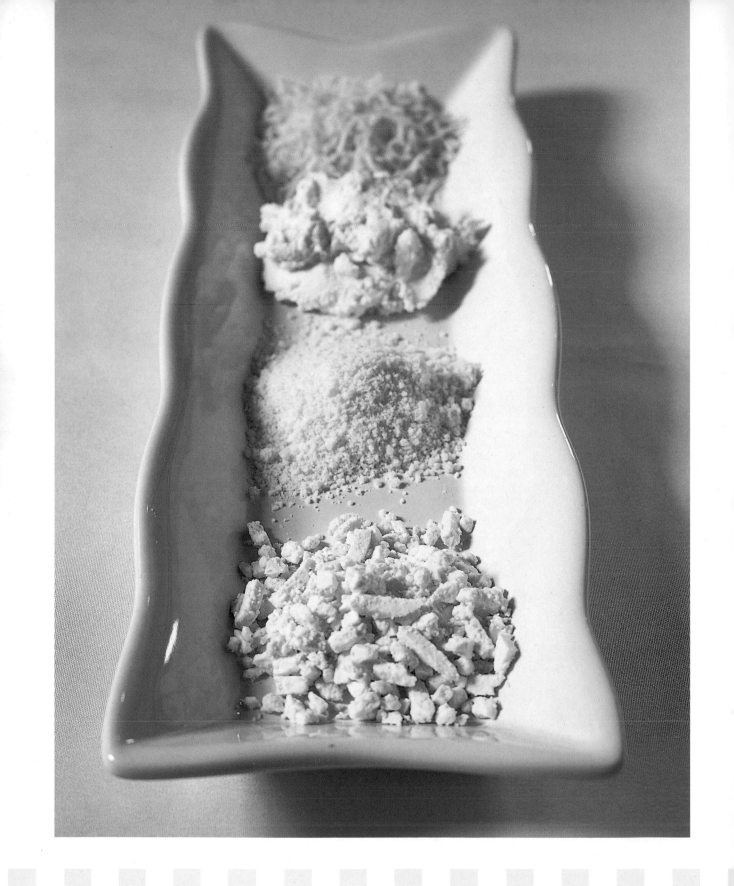

MAKING ARTISAN CHEESE